FIVE WEEKS ONE SUMMER

Martin Block

An illustrated account by mountain and alpine
enthusiast Martin Block of his solo journey to the
Swiss Alps in the summer of 2004,
with all photographs taken during the trip.

Pen Press

First published in Great Britain by Pen Press

All paper used in the printing of this book has been made
from wood grown in managed, sustainable forests.

ISBN13: 978-1-78003-347-1

Printed and bound in the UK
Pen Press is an imprint of
Indepenpress Publishing Limited
25 Eastern Place
Brighton
BN2 1GJ

A catalogue record of this book is available from
the British Library

Cover design by Jacqueline Abromeit

This book is dedicated to my parents,
Harry and Edyth Block.
Their decision in 1970 to ignore conventional wisdom and
instead take three young children
(my sister Alison, my brother Michael and myself)
on a road trip to see the Alps, was truly inspired.
In particular, I would like to remember my much-loved and
much-missed father.

Martin E. Block,
Birkenhead, November 2009

Map of where I went

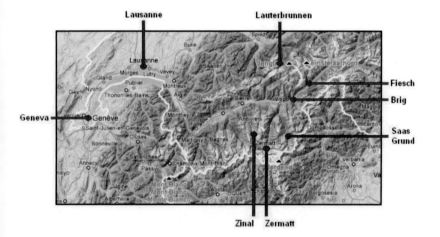

Why this trip?

A perfectly reasonable question but one which I find hard to answer. Mountains have featured large in my life since I was very young, as have the Alps which I saw for the first time at six years old when my parents took the family to the Swiss resort of Arosa (the trip mentioned in the dedication, earlier). I struggle to convey the excitement I felt on stepping out of the dark confines of our chalet, onto the hot balcony which I recall smelling strongly of wood resin, to look over the lake to the proud mountains beyond. As I aged, so my mountaineering aspirations increased, resulting in numerous alpine walking and climbing trips, sometimes with family or friends, sometimes on my own. But with the passing years came regret: the regret where you feel that you have somehow sold out on what was once dear to you, without replacing it with other things of worth such as a partner and children. This was where I was in 2004.

For years I had always had the idea of writing an alpine guide book for adventurous mountain walkers, and had even got as far as collating a target list of peaks, gleaned jointly from my experiences and stash of climbers' guide books. But it remained just that: an idea. Then in 2004, I decided to leave Cambridge to return to my home town of Birkenhead, to my roots so to speak. A flash of inspiration seized me and told me that this was the perfect time to research and write this alpine guide book, not least because it would give me a sense of pride at a time in my life when I sorely lacked this vital commodity.

So at 40 years old, with the monies from my house sale in the bank, I headed off on this extended solo trip to the Alps. The alpine guide book sort-of morphed into a diary on the way, as you will see; but the essential core of my trip remained unchanged, namely to walk in the high Alps and savour their beauty as I once used to do.

You join me now at Northampton Bus Station, where I've just been dropped off by my father...

Wednesday 21st July

Travelling to Zermatt

The coach stop at Northampton Bus Station is windy and ugly. The sound of passing buses booms off the bare walls. Just the Christmas before, my parents and I had stood here, shivering and severely stressed, waiting for our bus to Heathrow. It never came.

Today I have no such hassles and I board the bus as planned. This is all to the good because I'm really nervous about my trip. I've done long trips before on my own, both to Europe and further afield, and have spent a year living in Australia. But that was then and this is now, and I lack confidence. In the early 1990s, I climbed over 100 peaks a year, was out walking many weekends, had a full head of hair and weighed around 11 stone. Now I feel fat, unfit, uncoordinated, ridiculous and... old.

With that cheery assessment, I reach Luton airport, check-in, say 'Stuff It', and join the subtly-concealed and hugely enjoyable race across the tarmac to the waiting plane.

And so the trip begins. I pass through Geneva airport, buy a refreshingly cheap train ticket to Zermatt (via Brig) and board the train. The carriage fills with young school kids. No sooner are they seated than a couple of them suss out that the fold-away tables are really castanets to be opened and closed to great musical effect. I enjoy their tune and am saddened to see them leave at the next station.

Lake Geneva curves like a boomerang and I have the irrational sensation that the train's rapid progress around this curve is forcing me out of the left-hand window. Town follows town like records on a much-loved album – Nyon, Lausanne, Vevey, Montreux – while the lake glitters enticingly between the houses and vineyards. Life in the carriage continues to entertain. My percussionists are replaced by, amongst others, a sweaty, friendly guy who offers me some of his beer (a mate for life) before spilling it over himself as the train performs an impromptu lurch, and a gorgeous dark-haired girl who sits opposite me for many a happy mile.

We pass the Chateau de Chillon at the end of the lake and enter the Rhone valley. A bit about this valley as it features prominently through my tale – it is hemmed in to the north by the Bernese Alps, and to the south by the Pennine Alps; side valleys force their way southwards towards the Italian border, giving access to the Pennine Alps. I'm headed for one such valley – the Mattertal – and to the resort of Zermatt at its head.

Despite the great scenery, set off by some dramatic clouds, I spend much of the train trip worrying about the weight of gear I'm carrying. I've already had a nasty moment on the train: unbeknownst to me, I was sitting in a reserved seat and had to move, which required me to shift my gear and I nearly fell over as I tried to man-handle one of my bags onto the luggage rack. A whole trip of this would be a real pain. I decide to post back home as much stuff as possible, despite the cost.

Brig station is riotous. I leave it as soon as possible and cross the road to board the small train to Zermatt. This speeds along the Rhone valley to Visp, and then heads southwards into the mountains. At Stalden, a few miles beyond Visp, the climbing starts. I remember from past experience that at each steep bit, the train engine goes quieter and you hear a succession of clunks as each carriage swaps to cogged-wheel travel. The views are gorgeous. By craning my neck, I can see the prow of the Weisshorn and the sharp snowy point of the Taschhorn. The Matterhorn, Zermatt's most prized possession, appears only at the last moment before we pull into the station.

Zermatt feels the same as ever. I've been here many times and know it really well. You emerge from the station into a square full of people, horses (plus shit) and weird, milkfloat-like vehicles powered by electric motors. Cars are not allowed. Towering above this confusion are some of the world's most beautiful peaks, with the Matterhorn pre-eminent. I have to find the Matterhorn Hostel, my home for the next five nights; but first I need to eat and then action a cunning but cowardly plan hatched en-route, namely to stash half my gear in an overnight luggage locker to spare me embarrassment on arrival at the hostel. Isn't that pathetic!

I ask around for directions to the hostel and find it easily enough at the top end of town, across the river and about half a mile from the station. The hostel is built on the side of an existing hotel and overlooks the river. It's friendly but the atmosphere is more subterranean than the hoped-for Mediterranean. My dorm has half a dozen bunk beds, inhabited by a slumbering Japanese guy, some German cyclists, a Swiss bloke and an American called Brook. I take a bottom bunk, unpack my sack, jam this and its contents under the bunk, and then arrange and re-arrange my belongings to make it homely. Finally, I crawl into my sleeping bag and go to sleep.

Thursday 22nd July

Zermatt: Getting sorted before an afternoon walk to Findeln and the Grunsee

What a difference a night of sleep makes. I wake up feeling good and ready for lots of action. The hostel doesn't have much in the way of cooking facilities so I head into town to buy breakfast and deal with my excess gear. Zermatt has changed very little since my last visit. Everything is in the same place and I soon find the supermarket. I take my gear and my 'breakfast' to a bench by the town's tennis court and settle down to some serious sorting. The nearby bin does rather well out of this! Other items, such as cassettes, my binoculars and a scrappy pair of trousers, are destined for repatriation to the UK. I take these items to the post office, buy a box, and pay the hideous postage fee.

One of the things that I'd really looked forward to was meeting up with fellow hill walkers and climbers, with a hope to making friends. The Matterhorn Hostel – my current residence – is a standard backpacker hostel, full of world travellers who are sampling Zermatt, but not climbers. However, I know of the Hotel Bahnhof, just down from the station, which is popular with British climbers, so I call in there to see about rooms. The news is good: they have dorm-style accommodation at cheap rates and there is space available for me when I quit the Matterhorn Hostel in a few days' time. I immediately like what I see and book for eleven nights.

The day is passing and I still want to get into the hills. I grab my second bag from the station locker, sort some lunch, and then head back to the hostel to dump my stuff. Even in the daylight, the hostel feels dark and dingy. With all my gear in one place, I can now contemplate getting out for a walk. I pack a light bag, put on my boots and socks, and dash off.

Some 1500 feet above Zermatt stands the hamlet of Findeln, a collection of classic old chalets, hay lofts, a hotel and a chapel. It's a cracking objective for a short afternoon walk. In all my trips to Zermatt, it's been the first walk; a benchmark for fitness. I head up through Zermatt to its top end, then into the woods and the first of the countless zig-zags that I would climb over the coming weeks.

Wow! It hurts and I am sweating! I've been swimming a lot over the past year and have done numerous walks on the Cambridgeshire flats, but slopes are a painful novelty. I am conscious of my feet (my boots often rub) and my knees (I have damaged cartilage in both knees), and feel rather like a car hooked up to a diagnostic machine. I guess that my carbon dioxide emissions are off the top of the scale. And yet I enjoy it, knowing that a day will soon come when I don't feel so unfit. I force myself on, walking slowly and (crucially) not stopping, reaching the gorgeous Findeln within the recommended time. Quivering with effort, I sit

down at a café table and look out over the valley to the
Matterhorn and some of the other great alpine peaks, such
as the Dent Blanche and the Obergabelhorn. It all looks
fantastic and I feel spurred on for more action.

I decide to carry on to the Grunsee, a classic alpine lake-
cum-suntrap. The way drops down to a river then twists
and climbs through fresh, open woodlands that remind me
of the big forests bordering the Cairngorms. I am happy. At
the lake, it is all very entertaining. People are sunbathing or
messing about in the water or simply sitting and taking in
the view like me. Reluctantly I take off my much-loathed
boots to confirm my suspicions: my right heel is blistered,
so I decide there-and-then to buy a new pair.

After a paddle, it's boots on and back to town, to buy some
food and some kinder footwear. There is a water trough in
a small park in Winkelmatten on the outskirts of Zermatt. I
stop there to have a drink and to chill out before hitting the
town. Some French walkers are there also, drinking wine
no less! One of them tries to get his dog to leap into the
water trough, but it has more sense (than its owner?).

Shopping for boots is easy. I end up with a pair of so-called
trail boots, light on the feet but not as secure as proper
walking boots. Tomorrow, I plan a big walk up to the
Schonbuhl Hut, a mountain refuge behind the Matterhorn,
so I buy lots of food as well. Zermatt, like many alpine
resorts, has an open air chessboard. I pass it on the way
back to the hostel and am thrilled to see an elderly English
couple perched there on a seat, cooking their evening meal
on a stove with one of those foil wind guards wrapped
around the outside. This seems so sweet to me.

My dinner is cooked indoors, in the hostel's social room. It goes 'ping'. I remove the gooey mess from the microwave and eat it more with determination than pleasure. Brook, the American guy, is also eating and we have a good chat. He's travelling around Europe before starting work in Austria as a ski instructor. We talk travel and hills. After a shower, I pack a day sack for the next day's walk, watch CNN and then go to bed.

Friday 23rd July

Zermatt: hiking to the Schonbuhl Hut

The air is cool as I walk in the shade of the trees. My breath condenses in clouds as I plod and wheeze, conscious of both my laboured breathing and the gorgeous smell of wood resin. I am half an hour out of Zermatt, on the well-worn track to the hamlet of Zmutt. (At this point, dear reader, please join me as I stop by the side of the path, drop my sack first onto my knee and then onto the soft pine needles by my feet. Now let me show you inside. Yes, good, good... waterproof, food, water, head torch... but what is that bulky shopping bag? Pinch your nose before investigating further. The bag contains dirty washing, which I plan to deal with at the hut. This turns out to be a very stupid idea that means an over-heavy sack.)

The trees thin out and I find myself on a wide grassy terrace. Above are cliffs with banded rocks; below is a deep gorge through which flows a battleship-grey, churning river, carrying glacial grit from the arid Zmutt Glacier. The hamlet of Zmutt, sitting on this grassy terrace, is a smaller (and seemingly older) version of Findeln, my destination of yesterday. It really is of another century, with aged wooden buildings interspersed with cobbled tracks. I am here in good time, sweaty but pleased. The Matterhorn rises across the gorge. By the time I reach the Schonbuhl Hut, later, I will have passed behind this mountain and be able to see its most hidden side. But for now I push on to the next noteworthy point, Kalbernmatten, an isolated chalet that marks the halfway point to the hut.

Walking along the grassy terrace is refreshing. I am soon at Kalbernmatten, where I stop for longer to eat some bread and salami. In view is my next landmark, a stunning waterfall famous as a photographic foreground for the Matterhorn's north face. I set off for it now, capturing a rhythm at last, placing my feet well so that my movement is as silent as possible. At one point, the usual path is blocked by a landslide and I am redirected downwards on a narrow, stony path through straggly trees. Here, to my left, lies the wasteland of stones marking the end of the Zmutt Glacier, upon which the Swiss have constructed concrete buildings (to do with a hydro scheme, I believe) and driveable roads. It's functional, but not pretty.

I am back on the usual track and climbing up the zig-zags beside (and almost behind) the waterfall. The north face of the Matterhorn looks an awesome spectacle from here, towering two thousand metres above me. I stop to study it from bottom to top. At its base are rotten, decaying cliffs, down which fall streams of melt water from the upper snows. Above the rock cliffs are a band of precarious ice cliffs. Then the mountain takes a breather, giving as a concession a flat, glaciated ledge, bathed in infamy because it was the landing spot for those poor souls who died while descending the peak after its first ascent in 1865. Then the peak shoots up as the north face 'proper' in a breathtaking sweep of ice and rock.

The abruptness of the view hurts my neck. Tiredness is setting in but I desperately want to reach the hut in the recommended time. (A word of explanation: The path signposts contain the suggested times alongside the listed destinations. Meeting these times is a mark of competence and fitness, unless of course your objective is to linger en-route.) The path now gets stony and dusty. It crosses a plain of fine glacial silt into which my boots sink with a comforting squelch, and then passes a lonely, struggling pool that is surely doomed to disappear due to the constant influx of sediment.

I'm cheered by the final part of the walk. The usual path traverses along the crest of a glacial moraine, but this is blocked off (too unstable, perhaps) so instead I wander easily in the shaded dell beneath, eventually climbing to join the usual path at the far end of the moraine crest. Here it feels more truly like wilderness. The view opens out to include the Matterhorn's dramatic but shy neighbour, the Dent d'Herens. I slam down some sweets and psyche myself up for the final haul to the hut. This last effort takes it out of me, but by going slowly I stop only once and reach the hut in reasonable shape.

The Schonbuhl Hut is typical of its kind. It's a stone building, sited at 2700 metres, with brightly painted window shutters. As an alpine hut, it caters both for day-trippers and those who want to sleep over, either for a pre-dawn start to climb one of the big peaks or just to see the early light. I am outside on a large patio, sitting at one of five tables. Other walkers are already here, eating food or scanning the scenery with binoculars. New arrivals, like me, are lightly clad, whereas those who have been here longer are kitted out against the clearly worsening weather. Eventually, my breathing settles down and I feel able to enter the hut. The change in light levels is astonishing and everything seems dark. Slowly my eyes grow accustomed. I am in a stone porchway full of shelves holding clogs. These clogs are supplied free of charge like shoes at a bowling alley, for people to wear whilst indoors. Beyond the porchway is the main room, a carpenter's paradise of tables and benches. The walls carry shelving bearing wicker baskets that hold the belongings of climbers who are presently 'on the hill'. I studiously deny the existence of my lunch and buy soup and a roll from the kitchen, to eat outside while enjoying the view. So who cooks the soup and sells it to me? The answer is the hut staff, members of the club who own the hut; they live and work in the hut throughout the summer months, providing a service for walkers and climbers alike. I've been to this hut three times before, sleeping over on one occasion, and the view is well-known to me. Nevertheless, it still impresses massively and I spend a considerable time casting my eyes over the camera-shy back end of the Matterhorn and the ice cliffs of the Dent d'Herens. The view back down the valley is not so great as it takes in the sad moraines of the Zmutt Glacier.

The weather looks worse and worse, with a rising wind adding menace to the uniform, battleship-grey sky.

Washing my clothes isn't going to happen; I only hope that my dirty socks have enjoyed the walk. I head off, carefully picking my way down the zig-zags to the top of the moraine, then stride down the easy path beyond in a race against the impending rain. I'm playing leap-frog with two French women who are also Zermatt bound. At Kalbernmatten, I pass a family who are debating whether to stop for a drink.

And then comes the rain. Zmutt appears as a blur in the distance. I speed on towards this haven, suspecting (correctly) that I'd nip into the café to dry off and have a coffee. This is easier said than done. The French women and I reach the café together, only to find the entrance well-hidden up a slippery stairway running with rain water. At last we make it indoors. It's steamy inside but warm and homely. I take off my sodden cagoule and let it drip contentedly off the back of my chair; my sack I jam under the table so that it doesn't trip up the dashing waitresses.

A coffee later, I emerge refreshed, ready to tackle the curving track down through the woods to Zermatt. Perhaps it's walking through woods in the rain, or maybe the way the run-off has collected the pine debris on the path into sinuous ridges, but it all reminds me of Beddgelert forest in Snowdonia. I am shattered but really, really pleased with both my performance and the day as a whole.

Back at the hostel, I clean myself up and then chat with a lovely Japanese girl who is in the bunk above me. She gives me an apple! After dinner, I call my parents, a regular occurrence that makes me feel safer and hopefully stops them from being too concerned. My dad has decided to buy another car – a manual one after some years of driving an automatic. These chats were to do me the power of good and, along with emailing friends from Internet cafés, became an integral part of the trip.

Saturday 24ᵗʰ July

Zermatt: doing washing and feeling unwell

This is to be a rest day with clothes washing its principal activity. I wake up feeling rather tired. One reason is that one of the guys in the dorm has a bad cough and got up in the middle of the night to search in his rucksack. I was awoken in the dark by the sound of mouse-like rustling.

After breakfast, I head through town to the campsite at the far end. I've stayed here many times before and know that it has sinks for washing gear and lines to hang up drying. As I walk down the main street, I realize with a certain amount of pride that I am the scruffiest person around. I really do feel like a tramp.

What can you say about washing gear? Well, soap and cold water removes the worst stains and any obnoxious smells, but freezes my hands to a painful degree. I hang everything up on the line and settle down for a read. Then it starts to rain. Sitting around is damp and uncomfortable, even under the plastic sheeting that shelters the washing line, so two frozen hours later, I pack up the still-sodden clothes and relocate to a nice, warm café.

So the day is spent playing cat and mouse with the rain, trying to get the gear as dry as possible before returning to the hostel. I finally give up about five o'clock. Back at the hostel, Mr Noisy's bunk is empty (great). My American friend Brook has left also, leaving me a parting gift of a blanket bag, a really kind gesture. I was to use this for much of the trip.

That evening, walking through town, I sense some 'happening' outside one of the main hotels. The staff line up outside, presumably to greet someone famous: a film star? maybe royalty?? I hang around to await developments. A succession of milk-float taxis arrive carrying serious quantities of luggage, followed by guys with wary eyes who walk purposefully around the outside of the building. Next, a group of beautifully attired Arabic ladies emerge from the hotel and walk towards the station, to greet the arrivals perhaps? This is an incongruous scene for Zermatt, with its more usual population of camera-laden tourists, climbers, skiers and odd scruffy itinerants like me, but it is both colourful and entertaining. At last, I am freaked out that one of the security guys is eyeing me up so I leave feeling the same inexplicable guilt as when passing through customs. (Some days later, I spotted the 'security guy' driving a taxi.)

I do not see the royal arrivals. Instead I pop into a bar to warm up and have a beer. This is hard to get down (a bad sign). Eventually I empty the glass and wander back to the hostel. I feel dreadful (a very bad sign). Once in, I start shaking and every joint in my body aches and I cannot get comfortable (a very, very bad sign...). With weary resignation, I accept that I've caught something flu-like. My last thought as I lie sweating and shivering in my sleeping bag is that if I needed to throw up, I would do it in my old climbing boots as a penance for all their blistering.

Sunday 25th July

Zermatt: in bed and not well!

When I left work back in June, my colleagues kindly gave me a stack of tokens for Blacks, the climbing shop. I went to their Peterborough branch one afternoon and spent the lot, mainly on safety stuff for the trip. Two such items were a mini torch and a first aid kit. I now need to use this stuff. It is my turn to rustle in the middle of the night. I raid the first aid kit for pain killers. All the long night, I toss and turn in a futile effort to get comfortable, so much so that the poor guy in the top bunk must think that he's sleeping on a washing machine.

My sea-sick companion arises without incident or comment. Myself, I stay in bed for much of the day. Outside, the sun is cracking the flagstones on what proves to be one of the few totally clear days of the trip. I'd planned to climb the Mettelhorn today but this was obviously going to have to wait. Late afternoon, a guy from Arizona came in and we chat for a while, which cheers me up.

Monday 26th July

Zermatt: still not well, but a house move to Hotel Bahnhof

The hostel provides breakfast (for a small fee) and I'm glad to have a decent feed. I am due to check out by 10 a.m., but I still don't feel great and request to stay put until lunchtime. The hostel owner is extremely kind and lets me stay until 1 pm without paying extra.

At midday, I can stand my sleeping bag no longer. I get up, have something to eat and drink, and then assess my situation. The hostel is dark, empty and lifeless, and I decide to make the move to the Hotel Bahnhof even though I feel rough. My plan is to take a taxi, but I've no idea of a phone number to call and there is no-one around to ask. Eventually, I go outside to ask some builders whom I'd heard working on the house next door, and they point out to me a big advert (for taxis) plastered on the house opposite. Sorted! With great glee, I pack up my belongings except for the old boots and my sleeping bag, which I chuck in a bin just outside the hostel. The taxi duly comes and speeds me through town to the Hotel Bahnhof.

The Hotel Bahnhof is run by a lovely lady called Katherine. It's a four-storey building with an assortment of rooms, a basement and an attic. The basement houses a large kitchen, a common room, washing machines and a gear stash. The attic has been converted into an open plan dorm for low-budget punters like me. It is to this attic that I now slog, gritting my teeth, hauling myself and my gear up the many flights of stairs. The final flight is a steep, wooden set of steps (OK, a ladder).

This attic is my home for the next eleven nights. My allotted mattress is at the far end, under a window overlooking the town and the mighty Matterhorn. For storage I have a portion of wooden plinth at my feet, plus a similar space behind my head. My neighbour (the first of many during my sojourn here) is an excitable and friendly Japanese chap. Please understand that this set-up suits me fine and I am very happy with my new lodgings. The common room and kitchen together ensure that I would have some companionship.

I sort my gear, make my 'pit' as homely as possible, and then settle down to rest for the afternoon. Food is in my thoughts and I have this bizarre pregnancy-style craving for Frosties and milk. Unfortunately, I guess I have neither rested nor drunk enough and consequently am ill during the night. Can I say a sincere thank you to all the lovely people who helped me that evening, and apologise to the young English girl with lovely locks of hair who was a wee bit frightened of stepping over the legs of some weird guy sitting on the floor outside the toilet.

Tuesday 27th July

Zermatt: a quiet day to recuperate

It is a shadow of a man who contemplates his bowl of Frosties and milk this morning. I feel weak and small, and am not a happy bunny. I also feel that I'd made a fuss the night before. During the previous evening, I'd run into Brede Arkless, a mountain guide whose daughter Denise I knew very slightly from North Wales. Brede and I chat over breakfast, before she heads off with her client to Saas Fee. (An aside – July 2008 – I am very saddened to learn that Brede Arkless died back in 2006. A fascinating and moving obituary written by Jim Perrin for the *Guardian*, is easily found on the Internet.)

I spend the day very quietly, sitting in cafés and taking it easy. This is an expensive pastime and I start to worry about cash. I feel like going home. Instead, I buy Katherine a bar of chocolate to say thanks for her kindness the previous evening.

That evening, things improve. In the kitchen I get chatting to some of the people staying in the hotel. Chris and Martin are two climbers who are nearing the end of their trip. Chris is a fireman from Newcastle (we both reckoned that we'd met before) while Martin is the warden at Wasdale Youth Hostel. They prove to be great company. There is an Australian guy called Peter and a friendly bloke full of character called John France. And there is Walter, an Austrian mountain guide who looks like a nutty professor (or, as I revisit this text some years later, like Neil Oliver, the presenter of the TV programme 'Coast'), but who leaves me in no doubt that he'd be superb company on the hill.

My Japanese neighbour has had a great day (I think). I retire to bed early, fold my blanket over me, check that the mini torch is handy (for nocturnal loo trips) and that I have drunk enough water, and finally settle down to sleep.

Wednesday 28ᵗʰ July

Zermatt: a cable car trip to the Schwarzsee

I have to get out of Zermatt. Another day in the town, sitting in cafés or wandering the streets, would drive me mad... and then home to the UK. It's a beautiful day so I decide to splash out on a cable car trip to the Schwarzsee, a touristy but fantastic lake at the foot of the Matterhorn. I've been here countless times before and know it to be a great place to chill out and admire the awesome ring of peaks surrounding Zermatt.

On the way, I stop at the supermarket to grab the day's food. By sheer good fortune, I run into Trevor Tuddenham, a friend from my professional world of technical authoring. He and his partner are stopping in one of the hotels and we arrange to meet up that evening. My most notorious 'meeting up' on holiday was crashing into my brother on the streets of Innsbruck back in 1980. He was on a low-budget InterRail trip (and by 'low budget', I mean 'low budget'), while I was based in Mayrhofen with Venture Scout friends. Anyway, some of my friends met him first and gave me advance warning that 'your kid is in town' (we all being Scousers). It was great but too much to take in and our meeting was consequently rather low key.

These reminiscences amuse me on the cable car ride. At the top, I step out into the glaring sun, but more importantly into the world that I have so longed to revisit. I scuttle around with a light heart, then wander down to the lake with its famous chapel to chill out and take photographs, and finally climb up to higher ground to sit and admire the view.

From my perch, I look over Zermatt to the mountains that hem in its valley. On the far side, to the right, is the long skyline of the Mischabel, a ridge of peaks topped by the triangular duo of the Dom and the Taschhorn. Working around rightwards (to the east), I take in the punctuated skyline of peaks that have grown so familiar to me over the years – the Alphubel, Allalinhorn, Rimpfischorn and Strahlhorn – to stop dead at the great mass of the Monte Rosa. This peak, really a massif of summits, is the highest point in Switzerland (and the second highest in the Alps after Mont Blanc). I was fortunate enough to climb it in 1984 with my brother and one of his pals. The Monte Rosa is a remarkably symmetrical mountain from this angle, shaped rather like a Bedouin tent and looking very white and imposing. Carrying on round, there stands the bold Lyskamm with the Breithorn coming next. Any further twisting and I will need a chiropractor to unscrew my neck, so I turn around bodily, to the right, to see behind me the wasteland of stones leading to the base of the Matterhorn. That is enough for my long-suffering spine. Now back the other way, to my left, where I can see the peaks on the other side of the Zermatt valley: the beautiful Obergabelhorn, the ridiculously sharp Zinal Rothorn and finally, the stunning white wedge of the Weisshorn.

I walk a short way up the path towards the Matterhorn, along the much-recommended route to the Hornli Hut (the hut used by Matterhorn aspirants), mainly to try and recapture some of my fitness. Things are not too bad on

21

that score. One peak I haven't yet mentioned: the Dent Blanche, a favourite of mine and a giant amongst alpine peaks with its famous ridges and Andes-style snow flutings. This is the neighbour to the Obergabelhorn.

After a lovely time, I head back to the cable car station and downwards to the valley. In the cable car is a Japanese guy who has just climbed the Matterhorn. This is no mean achievement. The Hornli Ridge, up which most Zermatt-based climbers try their luck, is loose and very busy. It's a place for fitness, competence and a very cool head. My brother has done it, as have some Bangor friends. I feel confident on my return, enough so to prepare for an ascent of the Mettelhorn the next day. This is a big deal – 1800 metres of climbing – but I reckon I have to get back into the mountains. I buy chocolate, sausage, bread, crisps and fruit. For breakfast, I get a tub of yoghurt. Drink is simple: water from the tap.

In the evening, I visit Trevor and company in their hotel, joining them at the dinner table (though not eating anything). We have a really good natter and compare notes on our respective trips: mine just starting; his coming to an end. I leave the gathering in good spirits and return to the Bahnhof, finishing off the day with a chat in the kitchen.

Thursday 29ᵗʰ July

Zermatt: climbing the Mettelhorn

It's 6:30 in the morning: cold, fresh, invigorating and horribly early. My goal today is the Mettelhorn, at 3408 metres one of the highest walking peaks in the Alps.

I've done it three times before and this familiarity helps me choose it as my first peak of the trip. The mountain, an offshoot of the Zinal Rothorn, stands directly above Zermatt and casts its shadow over the resort. To reach the top, one climbs first up the beautiful Trift Gorge, past the Hotel Edelweiss, to the Hotel Trift at 2300 metres. Then the route enters a high mountain glacier-carved basin, reaches a col at its head, and then crosses a short snow field to the final, thimble-like summit cone. The ascent is one of Zermatt's big walking itineraries and regarded as a 'good tick'.

I spot the innocuous footpath sign to Trift and now join battle with the steep, winding alley leading out of Zermatt. Going steadily, I quit the town, cross the bridge over the foaming torrent issuing from the gorge, and put my head down for the brutal zig-zags up to the Hotel Edelweiss. At one point, these pass under a bulging rock wall where people have erected small memorial crosses adorned with motifs and photos of beloved ones – a sober reminder of mortality.

I am amazed and gratified at how I feel. Yes, I'm sweating and breathing hard, but I'm going strongly and feel good. Memories flood back as I walk by the precariously perched Hotel Edelweiss and head into the gorge proper. The path has the cheek to lose height as it passes through lovely trees. Then it thinks better of this and climbs remorselessly up the side of the gorge. Another torrent crossing; some long, lazy zig-zags; and then the final ups and downs to the top of the gorge; and I reach the Hotel Trift, collapsing gladly onto one of its outside benches. I must look like a beached whale.

The Trift Hotel is such a fabulous place, one of my top spots, anywhere. It is still early and the owner and his kids are setting up the outside tables for breakfast. Looking back the way I've come, Zermatt is lost somewhere down below but the far side of the valley is visible though still in shadow. I see the railway leading to the Gornergrat Hotel, easily identified with its two copular-like towers (so shaped as they house astronomical telescopes), behind which is the huge, emphatic marquee of Monte Rosa. Turning round to see the way ahead, there is a large grassy basin leading into the mountains, topped by screes, glacier and then the graceful tower of the Obergabelhorn. Chris and Martin, fellow Bahnhof tenants, had the night before recommended the home-made iced tea. This duly arrives in a pint glass and is absolutely gorgeous with its sharp taste and floating bits of fruit. Refreshed, I fill up the water bottle and then snatch some food before pushing on.

Now I'm well above the Trift Hotel, having climbed up past a waterfall into a magical upper valley, hidden from both Zermatt and Trift. At its epicentre is the most remarkable flat area, like a recently watered tennis court awash with pools of water and mountain plants. This surely used to be a lake? I stop to take a picture of this much-loved and well-remembered spot, only to find that the film in my camera has worked loose and will not wind on properly. I am angry and upset: the view is stunning, the weather also, and I have spare rolls of film sitting uselessly down in the valley. Eventually the richness of the scene cools me down and reminds me of my good fortune to be here.

The path becomes rockier and I have to pick my way along, playing the game of silence with my feet (the less noise made, the better the foot placement). A huge dome of rock stands to my right: the Plattenhorn, neighbour and pretender to the still-hidden Mettelhorn. As I watch my feet, I notice that the stone abruptly changes colour from red to white. The route flattens out onto a level ridge. Here I stop to grab some food, don sunglasses and rub suncream on to my exposed skin. I also look around. Looking back, I am high enough to survey the hidden valley I've just walked up, over Trift, to the Matterhorn and Dent d'Herens. Looking onwards, I see the path climbing up a loose, scruffy spur before it crosses a snow slope to the col. Peering over the col is the priceless, supine wedge of the Weisshorn, a sight of striking beauty against the rich blue sky. Bugger the bloody camera!

The final climb to the 3100 metre high col is hard work as altitude and fitness (or the lack of it) take their toll. The small stones on the spur are like ball-bearings, so I up my game and take extra care. The same care is required on the narrow traverse path through the snow. Meanwhile fitter parties that made later starts from Zermatt (or Trift), pass me by.

Everyone stops at the col; it's that sort of place. I arrive there in very poor shape. The way forward, across the rising snow field to the final cone of the Mettelhorn, is obvious and presents no technical problems, it being well-trodden and populous. I can actually see the summit sprouting tiny figures, their scale giving a depressing reality check as to the work ahead. Crossing the snow field, I slither a bit in the slushy furrow of the path, but soon I'm standing at the foot of the summit cone. I step off the snow onto the rocky path, kick a luckless rock to remove any compacted snow from the cleats of my boots, and head off up yet more zig-zags, this time of the steep-and-stony kind.

The summit appears just in time, the final 200 metre climb up the cone having being really brutal. The top is a small area of naked rock, a mini Tryfan, Slight Side or Hopegill Head. There isn't a lot of space so I shuffle around on my bum, taking care not to barge fellow summiteers over the edge. The 1800 metre drop to Zermatt is sickening.

Eventually, I stand up and take in the justly famous view. The Mettelhorn is high enough to feel amongst the big peaks surrounding Zermatt. Pride of place must go to the Weisshorn, which is seen at its best from here. From this angle, it looks like a colossal triangular 'half' of toast sitting in an invisible toast rack, with just enough asymmetry to give it character and beauty. The Matterhorn also looks impressive, but from this vantage point seems a little chunky for me when compared with its profile from, say, the Gornergrat. I can just peep over its left-hand side, into Italy. Down the valley, I see the familiar but beautiful peaks of the Bernese Alps: the Jungfrau, Monch, Aletschorn and Finsteraarhorn to name but a few.

It is now midday, high time to be on the move so as to avoid the all too common bad weather in the late afternoon. I pick my way carefully down the summit rocks, descend the scree zig-zags of the cone and cross the snow field back to the col. After a stop there for food and water, I tackle the trickiest parts of the descent: the snow slope and the rocky spur with its ball-bearing stones. The new boots cope fine, gripping the ground well and not rubbing my heels.

By now I'm really, really tired and just want to get back to Trift for another restorative iced tea. I can see the hotel, lying far below amidst the grassy hummocks. But between me and this oasis is a lumpy, stony path that requires good footwork for safety. Concentrating on my feet and willing myself not to look up, I find that the distance shrinks and soon enough I'm able to loosen up and stride out over the last few hundred yards of easy ground to the hotel's welcoming tables.

Trift is far busier than earlier. The owner has erected a telescope and is peering through it, up to the Zinal Rothorn (one of the big Zermatt peaks, standing alongside the Obergabelhorn above Trift), to try and pick out friends or relatives who are climbing the peak today, I believe. Others are eating, drinking, or just lounging around. Discarded sacks lie everywhere, resting against tables or just thrown with abandon on the nearby grass. I take mine and place it face down in the sun in an effort to dry it off. The black padding in contact with my back is soaked, while around it is a halo of my precious body salt that discolours the purple material. Nice! My iced tea arrives and the world is well.

I reminisce about earlier descents from the Mettelhorn. Many years ago, I was sitting at these seats having also just made a solo ascent. All of a sudden, there was a terrific commotion: a pig had broken loose and was charging through the tables and chairs, with the then-owner in hot pursuit. On another occasion, my brother and I were descending from the peak along with a Danish guy from the campsite. We were moving fast because the weather threatened storms. On the stony path down to Trift, I decided to pick my nose. Bad timing: I got it wrong and consequently had to walk with a hanky stuffed up my nose to stem the flow of blood!

Back to today. It's a hot dusty trek down the Trift Gorge to Zermatt. The pads of my feet are very sore and I'm dreadfully sticky. Eventually, I cross the bridge at the foot of the gorge, walk along the rutted track through the meadow, and hobble down the steep lane, cursing the uneven cobbles. The arrival into Zermatt from Trift is, as ever, abrupt and bizarre. I say this because the ancient cobbled alley literally dumps you in Zermatt's social heart, and you have seconds to re-orientate yourself to the thriving modern-day street scene. On my nose-picking descent back in 1982, we decided that re-orientation involved beers in the Brown Cow (one of the town's best-known bars), where from its dark but welcoming interior we emerged somewhat drunk after only a few beers.

So ends my first big day in the hills. I clean up, go out for a pizza to celebrate, and then retire to bed with very stiff legs.

One little tale from the past to add to the nose-picking day on the Mettelhorn. On our return to the campsite, my brother Mike got into the tent to sort out stuff while I sat outside. He proffered me a water bottle through the tent door, which I presumed he wanted washing out and refilling with water. I duly did this, finding the inside surprisingly dirty. When I got back to the tent, Mike took a swig, only to exclaim that this was tasteless water and where was the sachet of 'power-powder' drink he'd thrown in!

Friday 30th July

Zermatt: a quiet day

A quiet day, of necessity. After a late breakfast, I head into town to a café where they don't mind you drinking your coffee very slowly. This morning the music is superb, made up of so many favourite tunes, so I stay on to listen for a long time. In the afternoon, I go to one of the cafés to use the Internet. This is fantastic. I blast off emails to friends and surf the web for home news.

During the evening, Martin (the warden at Wasdale Youth Hostel) and I head out for a beer. I find him really good company and hope that he feels similarly entertained by me. One vital topic of conversation is the rigour of the climb up the Hotel Bahnhof stairs, to the attic. I am always shattered by the time I get to the final wooden steps – is it just me, I ask? No, he finds them tough, too, which cheers me as he is pretty fit. Martin and Chris are planning one last blast in the hills before heading home. For myself, I hope to do the Oberrothorn the next day, a peak very similar in height to the Mettelhorn but easier underfoot. This would be new ground for me.

Saturday 31st July

Zermatt: climbing the Oberrothorn

This time, with a combination of lighter sack, lighter boots and cooler air (it's 6 a.m.), I chew up the zig-zags through the forest to Findeln with relative ease. I'm still in the shadows, but through the trees I can see the Matterhorn, glowing like red-hot coal in the early morning sun. My thoughts wander and so I surprise myself when the cluster of Findeln's chalets suddenly appears ahead. The sun is directly behind them and they look spooky as silhouettes. I stop for water. No-one is around and it feels very special. With the turnoff to the Grunsee passed, I am on to new ground and sharpen up my act accordingly. However, the path to Sunegga is mellow enough to be driveable, a conclusion backed up by the number of chalets, cafés and the like along the way. I enjoy this super-simple, stress-free motoring on foot and feel that I'm going strongly.

Sunegga is the top station of a funicular from Zermatt, and the start point for the cable car to the Unterrothorn (the lesser brother of my day's objective, the Oberrothorn). Just below Sunegga is the gorgeous Leisee. As I sit and take in the view, the cable car station suddenly springs to life and a series of little four-seater boxes emerge from its doors to pass over my head. I drink some water and eat breakfast mark II. Debris from my sack lies strewn across the grass (why is the thing you want always at the bottom?), so I will need to make sure everything is repacked before I head off. But first I am going to rest up and check the map. The 'big picture' is to continue under the cable car wires to the next station, Blauherd, and from there follow the path round and then behind the ugly Unterrothorn, to gain the col linking it to the Oberrothorn. Beyond there, it looks fiddly: a rightwards crossing underneath the Oberrothorn's summit, then backwards and upwards to the top.

The next section to Blauherd, under the cable car wire, looks ghastly, so I head off rightwards on an alternative path known as the Marmot Trail, into a beautiful, shallow cwm. This is much better. I fly up, checking out the marmot information boards as I puff and wheeze along. All too soon, the trail ventures out of the cwm, onto one of its bounding ridges, and I see the Blauherd complex dead ahead. This is pretty ugly and I speed by as fast as my sturdy frame allows.

Unfortunately the path circling the Unterrothorn is in reality a gravel track, laid on for mountain bikers coming down from this summit. I'm not impressed and rate the aesthetics at 1 out of 10. I push on regardless, in the hope of better things, and find my reward once I get behind the Unterrothorn. An older couple are ahead: we smile at each other; I make a face and do signs to convey that it is hard work, and they agree.

The final 500 metres to the summit of the Oberrothorn is excellent, what with the track making cunning use of the ground and the superb views over the Findeln Glacier to the Monte Rosa. There is something about this final summit cone that reminds me of *Lord of The Rings*. I work my way up the traverse path, passing under the summit, to a completely unexpected lookout. What a fantastic place! It's a real gob-smacker, an eagles' eyrie, with huge, broken cliffs dropping away to the Findeln Glacier far below.

Everywhere there are small cairns on which people have placed memorabilia, perhaps of the fondly-remembered deceased. I recall having seen similar scenes recently on the summit of Ben Nevis, but I've never seen it before in the Swiss Alps – I like it. Also unexpected is an eye-shaped plaque on a pole, upon which are written words of peace (I think – my German is not so good).

It is now 10 o'clock. I'm moving up tight zig-zags on a dusty path of loose stones, to a destination as yet unseen due to the convexity of the slope. The hill has become crowded. At one point, where I stop to let a faster party go past and to have a breather, I notice that one of the men passing by has something like a small coin under his skin, near his collar bone. This intrigues me: if it is a medical insertion (a pace-maker?), then the guy enjoys frighteningly good health. Alas, I cannot follow at his speed and am left to choke in his dusty wake. Every so often, the path is broken by small rock steps. I try to retain my rhythm (at this stage of the game, after 1800 metres of continuous climbing, rhythm is all I've got). I put my right foot on the top of the step, place my hands on the surrounding rock so as to spread my personal burden, and then push upwards and move onwards. This goes on far beyond fun and pleasure, but I sense the surrounding slopes are focussing, coming together to their climax, and that my suffering will soon be at an end. I am right. The top appears ahead, a gently bowed crest with kind slopes on one side and a hideous void on the other.

People are gathered in colourful groups, sitting, standing, taking pictures, drinking and laughing. I'm not ready for any of this just yet; water is my first priority. I drink as much as I can spare (I've not brought enough, fool that I am). Then I notice a couple who are staying at the Hotel Bahnhof. We chatter. My breathing is returning to normal and I feel really good, despite concerns about the lack of water.

The view from the Oberrothorn is not as good as that from the Mettelhorn across the valley, though in fairness what I am seeing is blunted with heat haze. There is a feeling of space, of being on a high viewing platform with the world far below. All the usual suspects are visible: the Matterhorn, the Dent Blanche, the Weisshorn, the Monte Rosa and the Dom. Of these, the Monte Rosa catches my eye because of its grace and stature. The skyline between the Matterhorn and the Dent Blanche lies at the same level as me, and I can see over it to the jumble of peaks separating Zermatt and the Mont Blanc range. Mont Blanc itself is not visible. The famous Haute Route (a week-to-ten-day expedition for skiers and mountaineers) crosses this country on its way from Chamonix to Zermatt. I turn around and wander over to the lip of the precipice. This is a breathtaking drop, emphasised by the steam-like clouds which born by the upward drafts, rise up in my face. Far, far below is a stony valley, with on its farther side glaciers blending into the proud peaks of the Allalinhorn and Rimpfischhorn.

A Russian guy takes my picture. I must look a strange sight with my stained white shirt, mirrored sunglasses and floppy green sunhat. Two knobbly knees appear below a pair of green shorts. My ensemble is rounded off with red walking socks, folded down as far as possible to keep my legs cool.

I head back down. It would have been great to stay longer and try to get more from this place, but the lack of water is a worry and I want to reach Blauherd (a water source, hopefully) before thirst becomes an issue. So I pick my way down the path, along the steep zig-zags, past the beautiful eyrie, to the much-loathed gravel track. Somehow it seems longer going down. I start to do my own zig-zags across the breadth of the gravel track, to break the descent and spare my knees. This is OK, but I am ever conscious that such meanderings put me in the path of any mountain bikers hurtling down from the Unterrothorn. I look behind frequently!

Thirsty and jaded, I reach Blauherd. The café is closed and I cannot find a water supply. What I discover instead is a rich seam of laziness and pragmatism from within myself. Before I change my mind, I walk into the cable car station and buy a one-way ticket down the 1000 metres of hill to Zermatt via Sunegga. I enter the dark and chill interior. The four-seater pods are on a continuous loop, coming up from Sunegga. One slows down in front of me and I bustle inside with the same unnatural haste as when stepping on or off an escalator. My sack is a royal pain, all straps and bits that want to catch on the door, but eventually I am in and settled.

The pod (plus its one thirsty occupant) is ejected from the cable car station. I travel in almost total silence, the only noise coming from the pod as it swings gently back-and-forth. Below is the cwm with its Marmot Track, up which

I'd walked earlier that day. All too soon, the Sunegga cable car station approaches. I ready myself and wait for the slowing of the pod and the automatic opening of its door. Looming concrete, the sudden shadow after the outside glare, a massive increase in noise, an opening door, a jump out quickly without tripping up, and a re-adjustment to a static world.

This feels right. I hit Sunegga's café and order the largest volume of water on offer. This goes down as fast as sparkling water can without hurting my throat, as does the next. I now sit people-watching, feeling horribly smug at my day's doings. Eventually, I pay up (ouch!) and make for the dark entrance to the funicular. This is a steeply-sloping contraption that runs down an equally steep tunnel to Zermatt. It is weird and, I think, a little creepy. Perhaps it is tiredness, but I am suddenly extremely cold and lonely. ABBA plays over the PA system. I am alone on one 'ledge' of the funicular. Beneath me, on the next ledge down, are a family whom I recognize from the café. We exchange smiles and then revert to our own worlds.

It is a joy to get out at Zermatt, to be in the sunshine again. I am momentarily lost and decide to have an ice cream while I get my bearings. Lovely! Back at the Hotel Bahnhof, I get cleaned up. This is an odd experience: as the shower water runs over my head, I can literally taste the day's exertions as sweated salt gathers on my lips before being swept to the turbulent, murky pool forming about my feet. Alpine hillwalking is superb fun, but it is a hot, dusty, sweaty game. I wash my gear and hang it out to dry.

That night, the kitchen is packed full with folk, each bartering for spare room on the cookers, plus pans and tin openers. I lend a Japanese family some spices, a not altogether altruistic gesture as the daughter is seriously beautiful. The spice offer breaks the ice (OK, spices up the conversation) and we communicate as best we can, what with their halting English and my total absence of Japanese. They are good people and I enjoy the contact.

Martin and Chris have now gone, but John France is back having climbed the Monte Rosa as an impromptu guide, leading an inexperienced but enthusiastic team of Greeks, it seems. He looks shattered and has that reddened-face look worn by seasoned skiers and climbers the world over. Saying that, so do I.

Sunday 1ˢᵗ August

Zermatt: Swiss National Day

I'm up late after a poor night, punctuated with noise and bodily overheating.

After breakfast, I saunter up the street towards what is becoming my regular morning haunt – a friendly pub/café where they play great music and don't mind me hogging a table for an hour or so – and write up the diary. Today my second coffee is free. My route descriptions degenerate into third-rate sketches, rather like travel directions compiled from a telephone conversation. Scale is non-existent (as is artistic talent) and the resulting curves and squiggles reach new heights of bizarreness. For anyone analysing these pictures, I suspect psychoanalysis would be their recommendation to me. This done, I head to the internet café opposite, in one of the bars, and spend a lively half hour surfing the net and sending off emails.

In the afternoon, I head back to the Hotel Bahnhof and sit myself outside at one of the tables on the patio. I get talking to three really friendly English climbers: the Applegate brothers and a friend of theirs called Andrew. They've been on an alpine climbing course in Arolla (a small but highly recommended resort up yet another of these Rhone side valleys) and have the requisite burnt noses and cracked lips as proof. We chat 'mountains' and have a good giggle. Their enthusiasm is infectious. There are also a trio from Norway who, I think, are finding it hard to claim their first scalp in the hills. Beside the patio, over a fence, is a small bar, and these guys have taken to leaning over this fence to order their ale. It's a grand life so long as you don't weaken. Unfortunately, later that evening, one of them does 'weaken' while cooking his tea in the Bahnhof kitchen. It is really hard to tell whether the cooker rings are on or off. One ring in particular seems to work on Mondays, Wednesdays and Fridays, then withdraws into a cold, useless state for the rest of the week. Anyway, this Norwegian lad tests the ring by placing his hand on it – and discovers the painful way that it is on!

Later on, I chat to John France. He asks me what I'm up to tomorrow. When I mention doing the Stockhorn, he asks if he could tag along. I agree with pleasure, suddenly recognizing in myself a feeling of profound relief as the Stockhorn, solo, is worrying me. We head into town to seal our partnership over a few pints of gassy beer, then burp our way back through the throngs celebrating Swiss National Day, and then sit outside for an hour to watch the legendary fireworks. These are superb. Rich, colourful explosions light up the night sky, their sound reverberating like pin-balls off the valley walls. In the distance, other displays, visible but silent, provide an eerie backdrop to the spectacle.

I experienced my first Swiss National Day when I was just six years old. My parents took 'Team Block' to a chalet in Arosa, eastern Switzerland. We drove all the way from the UK, staying with friends whom my mother had made while au-pairing in Germany shortly after the war. My father was German by birth so language was no problem (he was Jewish and arrived in England as a refugee months before the outbreak of war). Thumbs up to my parents for having the wisdom to see the trip's benefits; two fingers to all those stuffy people who said I was too young to appreciate anything. OK, so I did a crap in one of our German hosts' bath. However, I can clearly recall things like my first ever night under a duvet (I felt like a tortoise peering up at its shell), the smell of the chalet owner's perfume, the cows with their haunting bells, the build-up and subsequent let-down of travelling through Birmingham's Spaghetti Junction, the liberally signposted German city called Ausfahrt ('Dad, is Ausfahrt [German for 'Exit'] a very big city or are we travelling in circles?'), and of course the Swiss National Day fireworks. We watched them from the chalet balcony as they exploded over the lake. In all, over the years, we went to Arosa five times.

I go indoors, climb up to the loft space, negotiate the strewn gear to reach my bed, and then peer out of the window to catch the final sights, sounds and smells of this hugely satisfying day.

Monday 2nd August

Zermatt: climbing the Stockhorn

John and I step off the train at the Gornergrat. We amble over to the viewing area where we collect our thoughts and bearings, the train ride up to 3100 metres having given us no time to adjust. The atmosphere feels sharp, filled with a sort of breathless excitement due in part to our rapid 'ascent'. A local celebrity, our companion in the carriage no less, alights from the train. It is the St. Bernard used to pose with tourist groups for photographs. If it is anything like my parents' dog, then it would have been a quivering wreck during the previous night's fireworks.

The Gornergrat is a justly famous viewpoint and one of my favourites. It is actually a smallish lump at the lower (Zermatt) end of a long ridge which starts life here, runs up over the Hohtalligrat and the Stockhorn (our peak of the day) to end in the vast snowfields to the side of the Monte Rosa. This ridge divides two huge glaciers: the Gorner Glacier, which flows from the Monte Rosa down to Zermatt like an ice super-highway, with moraine trails marking out the lanes; and the less dramatic Findeln Glacier, beyond which stands the Oberrothorn. It is the sight of the Monte Rosa and its adjacent peaks, set off by the artistic swirls of the Gorner Glacier, which makes the view from the

Gornergrat so fine. Also, as an added bonus, the Matterhorn is at its sharpest from here.

The snowy Monte Rosa is still in shadow. Behind us, to the west, the mountains are rockier and their fiery colour at this early hour speaks to me of impatience, a wish for the snowy giants to the east to awake and embrace the sun. All very flowery stuff for a rocky trail and two slightly overweight mountaineers! We walk down the back of the Gornergrat, then over the undulating crest towards our first objective, the Hohtalligrat. I am enjoying having company. At one point, the path dips like a necklace to avoid an awkward portion of the crest, and in so doing crosses a slope of mixed rock and snow. Nerves hit me here as it is the scene of a past skirmish between me and a large boulder in 1984. I lost! I was standing on a snow lip, ready to step onto said boulder, when the snow suddenly gave way, causing me to drop and bash my knee. Today, I have no problem. The snow is still hard in the cold shadows and I pass the dreaded spot with ease by placing my feet carefully into the solidified footprints of my predecessors.

At the Hohtalligrat, John and I stop to have a breather and check out the way ahead. This is an ugly spot, crowned with a cable car station and a more-than-usual amount of attendant debris: empty concrete sacks, rusting wire frames and so on. I choose somewhere to sit down and promptly fall on my bum. My chosen seat is a plank on two supports. Starting to get the picture? Anyway, I stupidly sit on one of its ends and upend both myself and my perch as a consequence. It is impossible to struggle socially with John, but this unplanned foray into the physics of fulcrums further warms our friendship and, like many before me, I am happy to look an idiot in the cause of social advancement.

It is clear that the continuing ridge to the Stockhorn is tough. If I had been on my own, I would have turned back (God knows how I managed it back in 1988, guiding two lads). The way leads initially along a naked edge of rock, not unlike pork crackling, and then down behind, through an area of rock-fall to a defunct cable car station called the Rote Nase. Here I have to 'make like a chimpanzee'. The route actually crosses the wooden forecourt of the cable car station, which I reach by climbing a sloping wooden plank and then gingerly surmounting the perimeter fence. Think 'Snakes and Ladders' and you have got the idea. John is already there, shaving off the first of many pieces of marzipan that we would eat this day. We eat, chat, and then brace ourselves for the continuing route: a traverse path below the crest that looks utterly horrendous.

OK, joking over – can I go home now? The route is vile. John is ahead, giving scale to the vast, steep slope of debris that stretches below us, ending in the Gorner Glacier many hundreds of feet below. The path itself is perhaps a foot wide, snaking in and out of gutters. Now the path seems to shrink to nothing as it rounds a protruding rock. I move sideways and, like a sex-starved man, rub my midriff against the rock while my hands fondle blindly above in the hope of finding the requisite two points of contact!

For reasons that will become clear, this reminds me of a trip to Prague a few years ago. Mike Lates, a friend of mine from Bangor who now lives and works as a guide on the

Isle of Skye, decided to go to Prague for his stag 'do', along with some mates, which included me. The trip was a complete hoot. One evening, we were wandering around town when our way was strategically blocked by a gang of women. As we passed through the throng, they started touching us up! What a dilemma! I reckoned that this was a pick-pocketing scam. Did I hang onto my chastity and lose my cash, or did I protect my cash and let them have a good feel? Well, I chose the latter: I hung onto my cash and had some titillation in the process.

The path opens up once more. Suddenly John stops dead and indicates for quiet. One by one, a group of chamois appears on the rocks ahead, as yet ignorant of our presence. They wander downwards, across the path… and then they sense us and charge downwards through the screes. What a beautiful sight. Now the path seems less noxious. Eventually, traversing turns into climbing and we grind up the loose, indistinct zig-zags to the crest. Bizarrely, the surest guide is some black plastic conduit buried intermittently in the grit. Just before we 'top-out' behind yet another cable car station (this time, the Stockhorn station), I notice the oddest way-marker I've ever seen in the hills – an upended broomstick (?).

Things are mellow now. We are back on the airy crest, marching across slabs of rock and snow patches, towards the distant nipple of the Stockhorn. We walk and talk and I share my fears about reversing the traverse path. To the left, very steep snow slopes fall to the Findeln Glacier; to the right are cliffs dropping to the Gorner Glacier. The summit really is a nipple, an abrupt rock peak, perhaps 10 metres in height, rising out of the snows. By climbing that mere 10 metres, our exposure grows immensely and the actual top feels very small and vulnerable.

This is a real summit, a real mountain. I sit hunched up on a rock, with John slightly below, his face buried in a map as he susses out what is what. I wisely stifle the urge to interfere. The continuing ridge drops to a col and then merges into the snowfields that lead to the crest and the Italian border. One peak stands out clearly – the Cima di Jazzi – a glacier dome from this (Zermatt) side, but a huge rock wall overlooking Italy. Working rightwards, the Monte Rosa has lost some of its beauty but its proximity and sheer size give it great presence. Next come its courtiers: the Lyskamm, Castor and Pollux, and the Breithorn. Italy is all around us, so to speak. It appears over the ridge to the right of the Breithorn, and I can see the rock walls dropping from the back of the Dent d'Herens towards the (hidden) Italian resort of Breuil. Next up is the Matterhorn, which appears over our ascent ridge from the Gornergrat. It is less striking from here than from the Gornergrat, I think; a comment that applies also to the Dent Blanche and the Weisshorn. Near to hand, and across the Findeln Glacier, are the giant Dom and Taschhorn. Finally, to complete the circle, I have a unique view of the Rimpfischorn and Strahlhorn appearing over John's hunched frame.

We slam down some marzipan, take on fluids, and then pick our way carefully down the summit cone to the snows below. Carefully is the word. I notice a belay bolt sunk into the summit rock, presumably placed there for climbers who see the need to protect this short descent with a rope. I see 'the need' all too clearly, but we don't have a rope. These first few steps downwards certainly carry a serious health warning, but we pass them safely.

The walk back to the Stockhorn cable car station is all joy, a real leg-stretch after the tensions of the ascent. However, the tension is not yet over. John suggests that we return to the Hohtalligrat via the connecting ridge rather than along the miserable traverse path beneath. This is sound mountaineering judgement; but the initial snow descent, steep enough to warrant facing into the slope, would have been very 'necky' for me in my canvas trail boots and without an ice-axe, and so I ask to return the way we came. Thankfully, John agrees. And now I can't find the start of the bloody path! We know that it drops off the crest just behind the Stockhorn cable car station. My first foray is wrong. We climb back up, me panicking because my objection to the ridge descent becomes untenable if we can't find the damned path. Thankfully, John has a better feel for the land. Soon we spot some of the black plastic conduit and then see the legendary broomstick... and my bacon is saved. All is well again. We pick our way down and then start the long traverse back via the Rote Nase station, to the Hohtalligrat.

Our arrival at the Hohtalligrat marks the end of the hard stuff. We find a decent seat this time (no fulcrums, please) and celebrate our venture with yet more marzipan and the remainder of my food. Suddenly, both of us stop chomping. Behind the summit of the Nordend (the left-hand of the two peaks that make the Monte Rosa look like a tent), a huge pillar of cloud has developed, towering many thousands of feet into the sky. I've never had such a sense of the height reached by clouds. It is stunning and distinctly biblical.

With the calm that comes after achievement and exertion, we saunter along to the Gornergrat, each walking separately as so often happens at the end of a great day in the hills. I am tired and find the last little climb up to the Gornergrat hard work. John has also slowed. At the Gornergrat, we get in the beers and sit and chatter for an hour before catching the train back down to Zermatt. Unfortunately, the beer makes me feel even more tired and, worse still, grumpy.

On our return to Zermatt, we grab a cup of tea and then go shopping. John has offered to cook tea and we head out to buy stuff for this. I am in a foul mood (sorry, John, if you ever read this) and moan about the mounting cost of our purchases. Thankfully, on returning to the Hotel Bahnhof, this shameful manner leaves me as I help prepare foodstuffs for John to cook. It is gorgeous: Spanish omelette, salad and bread, with chocolate for pudding. Thank you, John.

Later that evening, we chat with a couple of English girls who are part of a university group conducting research on the Findeln Glacier. Home for them is a tent beside the ice, with the occasional foray down to the fleshpots of Zermatt. I force myself to drink lots of water and go to bed with a clear head (and a rapidly filling bladder).

All this talk of tents, drink and bladders reminds me of a tale I wish to share. Some years back I was going through hard times and my sister (bless her) offered to put me up for a while. This worked fine and I did temping jobs locally whilst living there. Unfortunately, my sister's house was just big enough for her and her three kids, so I camped in the garden whilst enjoying the facilities of the house. Well, at night, if I needed to pee, I did it on the flower beds. One day, my sister noticed that some of her plants were not doing so well, whereas others of similar type thrived. Time to come clean and admit my nocturnal toiletry habits!

Tuesday 3ʳᵈ August

Zermatt: the last 'quiet day' – one of frustration

Welcome to the only really poor day of the holiday. Thankfully it proved to be the last aimless day of the trip. From here onwards, I ensured each day had a purpose and the trip improved immeasurably in response.

But back to today. I mooch around town, spending time buying and then writing a stack of postcards. Then I call an employment agency in the UK to see if I'm still in the running for a job in Warrington, only to be told that I'm not. I end the day going out for dinner with John before his departure back home.

Wednesday 4th August

Zermatt: hiking to Trift

I wake up feeling positive. This is a surprise because during the night my neighbour inadvertently rolled into my 'space' and awoke me by playing 'sleep footsie'.

I say goodbye to John, grab a book, water, some cash and some suncream, and start the long haul up to the much-loved Trift. Once there I really don't do very much at all, just laze around on the grass behind the hotel, look at the view and think about what I will do on my return to the UK. (Any reader game enough to make it to the end of this book will learn that this decision would be made for me. My father died suddenly just days after my return.)

I treat myself to Rosti for lunch. It's basically grated potato that is fried and then laced with various extras. My version is laced with bacon and eggs and is gorgeous. In the afternoon, I wander around trying to eye up scenes for pictures but end up taking none.

My time in Zermatt is coming to an end. I am not sad about this, principally because I've been here too often and know it too well. Or put another way, it is too easy for me. My next port of call, Saas Grund, beckons. I wander down the zig-zags to Zermatt, stopping en-route to watch some rock-climbers on the overhanging crags under the Hotel Edelweiss.

Back at the hostel, I chat first with the Norwegians (one of whom had the burnt hand, you may recall) and then, later on, with Andrew (the Applegate brothers had gone home by now). He is really interesting to talk with. Andrew has the latest versions of the Pennine Alps climbing guides which he kindly lends me (mine being 30 years old), so after dinner, I bury my nose in them to find out more about my planned climbs in Zinal. Thank God I did. They make startling reading and cause me to rethink my itinerary in the name of safety. The Pigne de la Lé, one of my intended peaks, looks too hard for me as a solo climber; but instead I read of a peak called the Corne de Sorebois, a highly recommended viewpoint and a far safer bet.

The Hotel Bahnhof has a huge number of *National Geographic* magazines in its downstairs lounge. Serious pleasure! I feel a bit rough in the evening due to an incipient cold, so I thumb through countless back copies of the 'yellow mags' and revel in their articles. As a kid, my grandmother paid for my yearly subscription to this magazine and I now recognize my very first issue from her: one from the early 70s containing lurid pictures of a volcanic eruption in Iceland.

When my eyes tell me that it is time to hit the sack, I climb up the infinity of stairs (they are still a challenge, even now), mount the wooden steps to the attic, and bed down for the night. This involves me filling up my water bottle, pushing my gear on to the thin plinth behind my head, balancing my sack on this plinth in such a way that it won't collapse on me, getting my mini-torch near to hand, and finally lying down with my book. My neighbour tonight is an Australian.

Matterhorn north face from the waterfall
near to Kalbernmatten (on the way to
the Schonbuhl hut)

Dent d'Herens from the Schonbuhl Hut in worsening weather

Schwarzsee, with the Obergabelhorn behind

Halo of body salt on my rucksack

Up early to climb the Oberrothorn: Findeln in the early
morning light with the Matterhorn behind

Enjoying the view from the Oberrothorn
(Monte Rosa to left; Lyskamm in the centre)

A breathless start to the day: early visitors to the Gornergrat,
with the Breithorn (and an intervening huge drop)

Monte Rosa from the Gornergrat

Matterhorn (L) and Dent Blanche (R) from the Stockhorn,
with the ridge from the Gornergrat in the foreground

A huge column of cloud towers over the Monte Rosa,
seen from the Hohtalligrat

Almagelleralp Inn with the Dom and Taschhorn blanketed by clouds

Arrival at the Almageller Hut

My washing drying out at the Almageller Hut

The early morning view from the Almageller Hut is less than encouraging

Zwischenberg Pass: The elderly couple step onto the
'Stairway to Heaven'

Sepia view into Italy from the Zwischenberg Pass
(my photo does not do it justice)

Monte Rosa and its mighty east (Italian) face from the Monte Moro Pass

The gathering beside the bronze Madonna on the Monte Moro Pass

People enjoying the view from the Monte Moro Pass

Coming down from the Monte Moro Pass,
with the Mattmark barrage visible at the far end of the lake

River and tree beside the Mattmark lake,
remembered from my last visit here in 1989

Some members of the Mischabel from Hohsaas:
(L to R) Alphubel, Taschhorn, Dom (highest),
Lenspitze, Nadelhorn and Durrenhorn (low, rocky, far right)

Climbers gearing down having returned from the Weismiess

Phone box at Kreuzboden

Val d'Anniviers and distant Rhone valley
from the Corne de Sorebois…'villages everywhere'

Walkers chill out on the grassy Corne de Sorebois,
with the Lac du Grimentz in view

Chilling out at the laid-back Arpittetaz Hut: the tables and
benches prompt some wistful memories

Woodpile at the Arpittetaz Hut

On the path to the Grand Mountet Hut: looking back
at the wooden gallery (perhaps the length of a bus)

Grand Mountet Hut
with the toilet block just visible behind the fencing

Obergabelhorn from Grand Mountet Hut

Dawn from the Grand Mountet Hut:
the Dent Blanche purrs in the early morning light

Returning from the Grand Mountet Hut: Belgian trekking
party crossing the gutter, looking like porters on a
Himalayan expedition

Even Zinal has its crime problems: cows looking for an ill-secured vehicle

Lauterbrunnen dries out after a night of torrential rain:
walking to the Trummelbach Falls

Trummelbach Falls: looking downwards onto the frenzied water

Me at the top of the Eggishorn

Eggishorn: its world-famous view up the Aletsch Glacier
to the Jungfrau (left), Monch (centre) and Eiger (low; far right)

Thursday 5ᵗʰ August

Zermatt: hiking to Zmutt and then to Findeln

I awake to the sound of tyres running through puddles.
Sitting up, I see the rain coming down sure and steady,
washing the streets and refreshing the rivers, but also
putting pay to plans for a high walk.

No more sitting around Zermatt! After a leisurely breakfast
(bread and jam, washed down with some Lapsang
Souchong tea that John left behind), I don my cagoule, stuff
its pockets with a hat, some cash and some sweets, and
head through the town, bound for the café at Zmutt.

It is a beautiful walk and I am so pleased not to have given
in to the bad weather. I've been up this way before, on my
jaunt to the Schonbuhl Hut at the start of the trip. Now
there is less pressure and I can meander at will. The water
in the Zmutt river literally steams with vigour as it starts its
long journey to the Mediterranean Sea. What with the rain
and the mist, it all seems rather oriental. I am also reminded
of the path by the Nevis Gorge in Scotland. Perhaps it is the
association with bad weather – the gorge walk, coupled
with a trip to Nevisport, being a regular bad weather
option.

Unlike its Scottish equivalent, the track here is broken up
only by pine needles. Eventually, I quit the misty woods to
step onto the grassy shelf on which sits Zmutt. For the
second time this trip, I arrive at the café in pouring rain.
Again it is a haven. I am the first visitor. I drink a coffee,

and another, day-dreaming while watching the clouds part to reveal snippets of newly-whitened mountains. Feeling nourished, I wander back down to Zermatt under a strengthening sun. It is barely lunchtime and it would be criminal to waste the rest of this promising day, so after watching the Matterhorn through the telescope at the end of town, I decide to walk up to Findeln.

But first, food! I nose around for somewhere cheap to eat and score gold: a restaurant in the square opposite the church. For starters, I have clear soup. As I am eating this, an elderly guy whom I presume to be the owner, wanders around the tables checking to see if everyone's dishes are good. He first lights upon an old lady and starts to add extra salad to her already filled bowl. In vain does she remonstrate! Next it is my turn. A bottle of red wine is produced and a liberal quantity tipped into the soup. Wow, it is lovely. The whole experience, with the guy's obvious concern for his diners' well-being, is real fun. It is the sort of scene I associate with the Victorian English gentry who climbed in the Alps in the mid-nineteenth century. And then, out of the white noise of foreign chatter, an Englishman shouts across the restaurant to attract the attention of his wife waiting outside. It is to do with payment problems (cards not accepted or something), but the episode grates and it strikes me forcibly how imperious English can sound as a language.

The afternoon sun burns down on me as I yet again take the zig-zags to Findeln, my third time this trip. I have a glass of water at the café and sit people-watching, as solo travellers so often do. (Loneliness was only occasionally an issue on

88

the trip, and then typically in the evenings. Coping strategies included people-watching, carrying a favoured person in my head, and also being prepared to miss out many of the usual preliminaries in order to develop speedy friendships. This last point unearths sadness in my opinion, namely that such behaviour comes across as odd when practiced 'at home'.)

This evening, my last in Zermatt, I plan to go to the cinema to see a climbing film. Katherine explains where to go and I find myself standing in a long queue, stretching down some spiral stairs and into a fancy auditorium full of polished chrome. Standing close by is Gerhardt, a German guy who is also staying at the Bahnhof, though in truth we had arrived at the cinema separately. We join forces now. At the ticket booth, Gerhardt asks the price. The guy answers 24F (about 11 pounds). This really annoys me because, yet again, Zermatt prices are out of my reach. I am so vexed that I leave before hearing further explanation, and march back to the Bahnhof and its free supply of *National Geographic* magazines. I retire to my bed, more than ready to leave Zermatt and its tourists behind.

Friday 6th August

Travelling to Saas Grund

Everyone is woken very early by a French team who giggle and chat to each other as they rustle and rummage through their gear. I am less than impressed, though I acknowledge that my incipient cold involves a tickly cough which must be equally annoying to these people in return. So you can see I am in a great mood! To add a sense of foolishness to my current disposition, Gerhardt comes over and explains to me that there had been a misunderstanding about the costs at the cinema the night before: the guy at the kiosk had quoted for both of us. I'd left so abruptly that he'd not had the chance to stop me. Oh well!

It is an odd feeling saying my goodbyes to the Hotel Bahnhof and its owner, Katherine, but I am more than ready to move on and board the train down the valley en-route to Saas Grund. Two girls share the carriage with me. One of them slips to the loo, only to reappear a few minutes later with a larger than normal, hand-rolled cigarette. I register this with interest. Surely it's a bit early in the day for the wicked weed? Will they offer me a smoke, or perhaps a toke?? A teacher friend of mine was a head of year at a secondary school. One day, he had to deal with a scene involving a lad who had smoked a 'bong' (a device for concentrating dope fumes by collecting them over water) in another teacher's lesson. Other pupils, brought in to verify the tale, described seeing a white pall of smoke drifting up from this youth, to be trapped by the unyielding ceiling.

My two companions share their cigarette (without offering me a toke) and then alight at one of the sleepy villages en-route. I myself continue onwards and downwards, to my own, extremely sleepy destination of Stalden. And boy is it sleepy. I check out the bus times to get back up the Saas valley, to Saas Grund, and then sit in the station café with a coffee. It is beautifully quiet and I feel myself relaxing. Two young girls arrive (not the smokers!) and from the interactions which follow, I guess that they must be friends or relatives of the lady owner. She kits them out and then sets them to work, serving at the tables. It is a joy to watch their enthusiasm and, to be fair, their skill, as they deal with the customers. Overlooking the station is a huge, wood-covered mountain, a sort of book-end for the Mischabel ridge. I try to envisage how long it would take to climb this mountain but get too tired even thinking about it.

The yellow post bus arrives in the station forecourt. I squeeze my still-overweight sacks in to the luggage hold and then jump on board. For the next two weeks, I will use these buses a lot. Their yellow shading exactly matches that of the Piccadilly set of properties in Monopoly. On a more serious note, they are a crucial mode of transport for locals and travellers alike.

My arrival at Saas Grund is rather an anti-climax. Restaurants aside, the whole place is shut down for lunch. After checking when the Tourist Office opens, I grab some food and then wander around the place, trying to get a feel for it. There are three resorts at the head of the Saas valley: Saas Grund, which is the least fancy but perhaps the most real; Saas Fee, the famous one – very touristy and I think a little twee; and the jewel, Saas Almagell, the smallest and loveliest of the trio. You may well ask why I plan to stay in Saas Grund rather than the more attractive Saas Almagell. The answer lies in an overheard conversation in Zermatt, from which I picked up that there was cheap bunk-house style accommodation above a ski shop in Saas Grund. To establish if this is so, and where to find it, requires me to visit the Tourist Office.

Like the good old days, I place my two sacks on the pavement outside the office, sit on the one not containing my camera, and wait. It is no hardship. The office opens on time. I sort out the whereabouts of the bunk-house and also get the phone number of the Almageller Hut (my planned destination for the next day). Down the high street I march until I come across the Zurbriggen ski shop. No problem says the lady in the shop: the bunkhouse is behind, in a separate building, and the cost is cheap. I pay an advance and receive a key in return.

The bunkhouse is beautifully done out in pine but the hallways are incredibly dark because the lighting runs on timers – the sort you get in hotels, which leave you groping in the dark if you overrun the miserly time setting. Thankfully the rooms themselves are far brighter and quite cheerful. I am in 'Weissmies', a room with long shelves of bunks and a doorway onto a fantastic balcony that overlooks a puddle-ridden tennis court and the cloudy mountains. The owner says that others will be sleeping here this evening, which is good news as the room is far too large for one person.

After sorting my gear, I start on the obligatory clothes washing. I have a stinking bundle from my last few days in Zermatt and this needs attacking if people are to be sleeping within smelling range of my gear. Washing is easy: I nip into the shower room and do it there. Drying, however, is more of a challenge. For some reason, I choose not to put it out on the balcony, but to head back out and find a spot to do the deed. I'm so glad I make this choice as I shall now explain.

My 'spot' is the municipal park. This has a chain-loop fence on which I drape my clothes, in the manner of Tibetan prayer flags. The wind plays around my briefs, shirts and so on, while I settle down on the grass to watch the clouds play 'look-see' with the mountains. Two peaks stand out: the Ulrichshorn, an offshoot of the higher but invisible Nadelhorn, towering directly overhead; and the Mittaghorn, a lower but no less impressive summit that seems to block the onward valley. My father climbed the Mittaghorn when he stayed here back in the 1950s. All of a sudden, the park is invaded by two football teams: a group of handicapped children and their carers out for a bout of soccer. It is fantastic to watch, a most heart-warming episode. At one point, a lad boots the ball and it hits one of the carers in the stomach. Everyone just laughs! At another point, the ball rolls my way, to be chased by one of the handicapped children. He speaks to me in what is presumably perfect German, and I panic because I don't want my lack of language to be interpreted as a lack of understanding (if you see what I mean). Well, smiles and gesticulations suffice and he seems happy enough with my response.

The rain comes on and I retreat back to the bunkhouse, armed with my still-damp washing. I feel great after seeing the football match. With almost child-like enthusiasm, I book a place at the Almageller Hut, including dinner and breakfast, and pray that the weather improves. Next, using the same phone card, I phone my parents, a two-daily routine that gives me a lot of pleasure and hopefully reassures them of my well-being. Phone cards are a regular purchase and worth every penny. I also catch up with the owner, to tell her that I won't be back the next night. She is grateful to me for letting her know but advises me that I must clear up any stuff of mine left in the dorm and stash it in the common room. Later that night, as I lie reading, my dorm companions arrive and the previously frigid room suddenly glows with chatter and the universal sound of the rucksack-carrying traveller: rustling plastic. We chat and tell each other of our plans. Theirs sound very keen: they are in the Saas valley to tick a number of four thousanders (4000 metre peaks, an alpine version of the Munros) and they've already done a fair few. I am very grateful to have the company and just hope that my ticklish cough doesn't drive them mad.

Saturday 7th August

Saas Grund: hiking to Almageller Hut for overnight stay

Blast and bugger! What am I to do about the still-damp washing? If I leave it overnight at the bunkhouse, in a polythene bag, it will fester and stink. It looks like I'll have to take it with me, up to the hut, and maybe dry it there. Damn! Now it's my turn to rustle plastic as I squeeze a bag full of damp clothing into my sack. I find the common room (called 'Fletschorn'), dump the remains of my belongings into my second sack, and leave it there alongside other people's gear.

Now I am out of the door – at last. I stride quickly up the street to the supermarket, buy my usual breakfast and lunch staples (milk drink, yoghurt, bread, paprika flavoured crisps, chorizo sausage, chocolate and fruit), pay hurriedly at the counter and, with shopping bag in hand, waddle up to the bus stop. Why I hadn't the sense to do the shopping last night baffles me. The bus arrives and I feel my breathing return to normal.

Perhaps it's because I'm staying overnight at a hut or perhaps because I'm revisiting a favourite spot, but whatever the reason excitement and motivation pour through me. The bus drops me in the main square at Saas Almagell. It feels really, really good. There are a couple of benches ringing the square, so I choose one that offers a nice view and settle down for an unleisurely breakfast in full view of the inhabitants. Fifteen years ago, I did exactly the same thing as a prelude to exactly the same excursion: to the Zwischenberg Pass, overnighting en-route at the Almageller Hut. Then, I'd just finished two years as a secondary school teacher and to say that I was messed up would be an understatement. I spent four days walking in this area, literally sorting out my head, before meeting up with my brother and his wife in Zermatt.

After allowing perhaps two minutes for my breakfast to settle, I head out of the square, between the old wooden chalets with their window boxes draped with bright flowers, through the still-damp field rising behind, to the start of the day's climbing.

So here I am, zig-zagging up the steep wooded side of the Saas valley, to reach the lip of a hanging valley. And it is beautiful. I've been here before and remember it being good, but this is lovely. The path winds up between the trees, going teasingly close to the cascade pouring from the hanging valley above. Concrete... a bizarre alternative to the more usual tree roots and pine needles! To my surprise and disappointment, a section of the path is concreted, which should suggest safety but in fact has the opposite effect because its crumbling edge accentuates the sheer drop down to the valley floor far below. No matter, the comforting pine needles and tree roots soon re-appear.

It takes me about an hour to reach the waterfall at the lip of the hanging valley, from where I can spot, a mile or so onwards, the brightly painted Almagelleralp Inn. The river is bridged here, so I cross over (as instructed) and take to the lazy ups and downs of the path on the far side. This is easier going and I have energy to spare to enjoy both the walking and the view. Behind me, strafed with cloud and towering above all else, stand my two friends the Dom and the Taschhorn, the king and queen of the Mischabel. (Earlier this summer, on a flight to Italy, my dad and I peered out of the window and watched these two graceful giants slowly recede out of view while we were born ever southwards towards Florence.) Ahead lies the jagged crest of the Portjengrat, while directly above me, across the river, rises the stark cone of the Almagellerhorn, looking like it has been stripped of its skin. This peak looks tough to me though I know from past reading that there is a practicable route to its top. The rocks on its flanks have peeled off to expose a corrugated cliff, very much like the Atlantic Slabs in North Wales (at the foot of the Nant Francon, near to Bethesda).

With renewed energy, I eat up the stony track and arrive somewhat breathless at the Almagelleralp Inn. This has changed since my last visit – for the better, I think. As well as the expected tables, chairs and blackboard displaying the provender on offer, there is a kids' area with swings and slides and the like. Something about this set-up appeals to me. I decide that it is the sense of community which it engenders. One of the women working there fills my water bottle. With this done, I walk a few minutes further up the track, find a suitable spot to sit, and then lay out both myself and my wet washing. Food is taken and water imbibed. Then I get the camera out to take a picture of the inn, with its vivid red window shutters, backed by the Dom and Taschhorn, themselves dwarfed by huge dramatic clouds that suggest worsening weather.

That was three quarters of an hour ago. Things have changed. I am on the long zig-zags leading up the big grass slope to the Almageller Hut. Behind me, the Almagellerhorn acts as a yardstick to my progress and I am not going well. As I walk, a helicopter passes overhead, presumably heading to the hut with supplies. Its diminishing drone gives me an indication of how far I have to climb and I reckon it might be a long way.

On the plus side, the view is fantastic, the weather is holding out, and there are some friendly people playing leap-frog with me on the track, who will hopefully be staying at the hut as well. After a stop for food and drink (my response to everything, it would seem), I carry on, taking some comfort from the gradual easing of the gradient. In truth, this really is not steep and I should be cruising along rather than making out like a car with a clogged-up fuel pump.

The last bit is a nightmare. I can see the hut, perhaps 200 feet above me, with its flag blowing proudly in the wind. I can also see people looking out over the parapet: I can hear them laughing and chatting, totally indifferent to my presence beneath their line of sight; and I can see beyond the hut to the Zwischenberg Pass, smothered in a dark mass of cloud. Between me and sanctuary lies a small undulating patch of snow and then a steep bluff of grass and stones, up which the path leaps to the comforts of the hut. At last, I am there, at the hut. I feel absolutely wretched.

Truth be told, I'm in quite poor shape. I sit catatonic and disorientated amidst a group of happy, chatting mountaingoers. What to do? I'm not sure from where the idea comes, but it is a good one – I have a wash. The hut has an indoor toilet/washroom, so I steal in there and perform those Kama-Sutra style contortions associated with washing yourself while freezing your feet on a stone-flagged floor. For my more private parts, I retire behind a locked door and gingerly tip the icy contents of my water bottle between my legs. I would love to have a video of me hopping around, trying to dry myself with my dirty shirt while standing on other clothing to prevent the icy cold from the floor penetrating up through my body. And to quote Rhys Ifans from the film *Notting Hill*, my balls are the size of raisins.

I now feel much better. I wander into the main room (a wooden wonderland of benches and tables, with an amazing kitchen in which the hut staff are preparing tea), check in, return to the cobbled foyer, don a reasonably fitting pair of clogs (provided by the hut) and stash my gear. Then I venture outside, armed with my washing, to find a suitable boulder on which to spread this out to dry. The wind is strong enough to dispatch my underpants to Italy, free of charge, so I collect some rocks to weigh everything down.

It's a gorgeous afternoon. It just seems to go. I sit on the parapet, eyed so enviously on the way up, and look with smugness over the heads of other poor souls now sweating up those last 200 feet, to the awesome wall of peaks to the west. These are framed between the Almagallerhorn to the left (now only slightly higher than me) and the descending ridge of the Weissmies to the right. And what a wall! I can see all the peaks dividing the Saas valley from Zermatt; from the Strahlhorn, over the Dom and Tashchorn, to the Nadelgrat. To my right, partly blocked from view by the hut itself, is a long, spiked rock ridge called the Dri Horlini (sounds like a magician's act) with climbers visible traversing its crest. This is a popular rock traverse, more suited to the Aiguilles Rouge above Chamonix than to around here. Behind me is the brooding mass of the Weissmies, one of the four-thousanders and the most common objective from this hut, with the Portjengrat to its right. The Zwischenberg Pass – my destination for the morrow – separates these two peaks. Finally to my left, I can see the full length of the gently-graded glacier which runs from the Almagelleralp Inn up to the Italian border, backed by the beautiful Sonnighorn.

For entertainment, I sit watching the climbing parties as they progress along the Dri Horlini. One group obviously decides to 'bale out' and abseil down the cliff face. I am awe-struck by this as it seems to me that the component stages of their chosen abseil are longer than a normal rope length. Well, I'm wrong: I am spectator to an abseiling master class – swift and unfussy – and they reach safety without mishap.

On one of my forays around the hut's environs, I spot some technical papers floating in a pool of water, a bit like exposed photographs languishing in a developing bath. Nearby is their source: a fluttering heap of papers restrained only by a small stone placed on top, which is obviously not up to the job as it is letting go of the more agitated sheets. Also nearby is their owner (presumably) who is sound asleep, perhaps as a consequence of the papers' content. I fish out the wet sheets, place them near to the main pile, and try to weight everything down without waking up Sleeping Beauty. Unfortunately she awakes with a start to find me instead of Prince Charming. There are warm thanks but sadly no fairytale ending.

I'm in the first sitting for dinner and find myself seated near the back of the room, on a table with two women whom I recognize from the walk up, and a father-and-son team, all from Germany. The food is gorgeous, though I make a total fool of myself by stating that the chicken soup is very tasty (it being asparagus soup). The only thing wanting is fresh air – it is horribly hot and airless. I open a nearby window, only to reclose it with reluctance because it unleashes a gale into the room.

Fed and watered, we are ousted onto the patio to make way for the second sitting. It's clear to me that I must have a cold or something and to sit outside in the gathering cold is a bit of a pain. But as recompense, the views are spectacular, especially the clouds which steal the show easily over the now-sombre mountains. If this means good weather for tomorrow, then I'm the Sultan of Brunei.

Eventually we are allowed back in. I buy a hot drink and sit down, ready to be sociable. I don't wait long for a 'bite'. A nearby group, including the lady with the water-soaked papers, very kindly includes me in their chatter. They're from the Geneva branch of the SAC (Swiss Alpine Club). My lady-friend is English. The name has gone (I'm sorry), but she is great to talk with. She works at CERN near Geneva, where they do particle physics experiments, and was, at one time, the local chair of the SAC. I hear myself ask her for a job. Oh my God!

With the dinner things washed up, the hut staff take people's payments for the night. We stand in a line, brandishing cash and various membership cards, the latter in the hope of getting a reduction. I feel rough again. I'm reminded of the character Ivan Denisovitch, a camp inmate in Solzenhitsyn's eponymous book. My turn comes at last. I show my BMC (British Mountaineering Council) membership card and get a reduction, though in truth I feel that the full price is very reasonable. It certainly beats sleeping rough outside, as I have done so many times before on cash-strapped alpine trips.

I stay around a little longer, then admit defeat and head for my allotted 'bed': a single slot on the bottom bunk, in a room full of excitable teenage lads. This worries me for I suspect they may be noisy. Actually, it is I, not they, who will make a noise during the night. The ticklish cough is of the most irritating kind. I try everything – quiet little coughs, swearing, jamming the blanket down my throat, head-butting the wall – all to no avail. As I struggle, a storm starts. Lightning flickers but oddly no thunder can be heard. The room periodically illuminates with light and I can hear the rain pelt down hard on the stonework outside. I admit defeat and sneak out of the dorm for a cough and a pee. Down the wooden stairs I creep, clutching my little torch. I lift the huge latch on the main door, push it open as quietly as possible and, in a seriously miserable mood, add the contents of my bladder to the rainfall.

Sunday 8ᵗʰ August

Saas Grund: hiking to Zwischenberg Pass
from Almageller Hut

The weather has improved somewhat overnight so I decide to go for the pass after all, this despite having a head that feels like a football and the breakfast-time view of swirling cloud engulfing the hut. Two things get me going: the sight of an elderly couple calmly wandering past the hut, en-route to the pass, and that most tireless of motivators – guilt. And despite everything, I'm having a good time. The track is lovely, and while picking my way along it, through the slowly clearing mist, I feel pleasure. If I'm really lucky, the cloud will have cleared by the time I reach the crest of the pass (a thousand feet above the hut, and perhaps a mile from it in distance).

The grasslands, peppered with small stones, now stop abruptly and I am left standing in a wasteland of dark stones, interspersed with troughs of dirty, grey snow that looks well past its sell-by date. By pure convenience, nature has laid on a veritable stairway to heaven: a dark tongue that rises steadily from this toilsome mess to within a hundred feet or so of the crest. I step onto this tongue, not quite knowing what to expect, and find to my surprise that it is pure rock, rather like a solidified lava flow, with a black and gritty surface. I wend my way up its spine, passing the elderly couple en-route.

Eventually, the stairway can serve me no longer and I quit it to its left, along a path of the finest stones that give under my feet and sneak over my socks, into my boots. No matter, the going is fantastic and it looks like I will have a view after all. I reach the final, short wall and take to its zig-zags with urgency. Now the stones are large and angular with garden-centre gravel spread in between. My feet scrunch the finer fraction underfoot. The sound is exciting, as is the location, and my spirits build up like the pressure in a shaken can of beer. Knee up; hands for balance; careful footwork; look two steps ahead; keep a good rhythm; for God's sake don't twist an ankle.

I'm at the crest of the Zwischenberg Pass, shaking my hands with childish excitement, bobbing up and down to vent off some of the pent-up pleasure that has built up inside... but not fast enough. I find myself jumping up and down on the spot. What my fellow walkers behind may think, I care not. The view is out of this world, literally, with colours not normally found in Earth's standard paint palette. This is a faded sepia photograph: ridge upon ridge of craggy hills, each divided by delicate, faded mists, with as a backdrop the plains of Italy's Po valley, themselves covered in their own, brownish blanket. The sun is nowhere to be seen, thank goodness, for it is the subtlety of colour that lifts the prospect far beyond the mundane. In the far distance stands the Piz Bernina (above St. Moritz) with to its side the Monte Disgrazia which I climbed with Bangor friends back in 1991. The nearer view is no less dramatic. Directly beneath my feet is a giddy drop, at the foot of which, far below, lies a large snowfield that bends out of sight as it falls to the grassy Zwischenberg valley beyond. To my left is the nose of the Weissmies; to my right the uncompromising spire of the Portjenhorn, with cliffs that fall away in some of the most evil-looking buttresses I've ever seen. Behind me, the cloud is unrelenting and I can see very little.

Originally, this book was to have been a guide written for mountain walkers who wanted to climb amidst the big peaks without having to don crampons or stagger through fields of boulders in the pre-dawn by the giddy light of a head-torch (that is, be alpinists!). I'd researched a dozen peaks for this guide. One of them, the Tallihorn, looks across at me now. Between me and it lie lots of stones and lots of distance. It would take real commitment to climb it, more commitment than I can justify given my solo status. With this simple decision, the stuttering flame of the guidebook idea finally dies out, to be replaced by this diary. But I am not sorry.

The two elderly walkers reach the crest. We exchange pleasantries and then they continue on for a proper crossing of the pass. I'm intrigued to see their onward route because a direct descent to the snowfields below looks hideous. But these old-timers know their stuff: they climb a short way up the crest towards the Weissmies, traverse across its face for a bit, and then make their descent down its gentler snow slopes. Another couple arrive, this time from above. It transpires that they've tried to climb the Weissmies and are returning unsuccessful. I sense the tension between them: the one who was keen to carry on; the one who was not. I've been in this situation myself and it's hateful, with no third person to diffuse the atmosphere and plenty of time for reflection during the long descent.

I take yet more photographs and try to absorb a final, mental image of the vista.

Back at the hut, I seek out the warden to let her know that I am back safely. She looks at me as if to say 'so bloody what'. I grab the remainder of my kit, shove it in my sack, and then head down in the gathering sunshine to the Almagelleralp Inn far below, to fulfil a promise to my ever-demanding stomach for some more good food.

An hour of zig-zag bashing later, I'm at the inn, sitting at one of the outdoor tables. The sun is strong now, so I try to shift one of the weighted umbrellas to give me some shade. No go. I then roll it across in alternating arcs of motion, presumably to the annoyance of the other diners who had been perfectly at ease until my arrival. And so to the food – KaseShnitte – a version of Welsh Rarebit that is gorgeous except for the gherkin placed on top for show (I absolutely detest gherkins). The waitress I recognize as the lady who filled up my water bottle the day before. I like her. I eat up, pay the bill, and in my exuberance decide that we only live once so venture to tell her that she is beautiful. Romance-wise, I'm meant for another age, one in which bold knights climb towers and slaughter foe to rescue damsels in distress... and surprise, surprise, I'm single!

It is in the best of moods that I stroll down beside the chattering river, the tall snowy peaks towering ahead. In no time at all I am at the bridge at the lip of the hanging valley, ready to start down the steep trail through the woods. The smell of resin is strong. Every so often, I slow down to pick my way carefully across some exposed tree trunks. Suddenly a short, rocky drop appears, of which I have absolutely no recollection from yesterday's ascent. Beyond this, I step on to the concrete that so surprised me on the way up. This is a superb vantage point for viewing Saas Almagell, spread like a street plan in the valley far below.

The path quits the woods, crosses the meadow, and then turns into a narrow lane that snakes between the old chalets. Flowers are everywhere: on every balcony; in baskets hanging off every hook; and in the gardens, where they jostle for position with well-tended vegetables. This is a truly beautiful spot. I take pictures as best I can. The lane deposits me back in the main square, now full of life, with people bustling around, perhaps waiting for a post bus like myself or perhaps on a Sunday 'out' with their family. I check the bus times to Saas Grund. There isn't a bus for ages (for which I'm secretly glad), so I sit on one of the benches, reflecting on the trip as a whole and enjoying this time before my return to the less attractive Saas Grund.

Back at the bunkhouse, my room is locked up. However I can get into 'Fletschhorn', the common room in which I had stashed my gear the previous morning, so am able to find my shower things, grab a shower and change my sweaty clothes. Afterwards I read until the rooms are opened, at which time I reclaim my bed and start to 'make house' yet again. I go to the shops and buy some food for tea, which I eat by the side of the river in the evening light. I guess the pleasure of the day needs recounting and there is no-one there to listen to my tale, so it is in a fairly low frame of mind that I wander the streets. Popping into one bar/restaurant, I spot my companions from the dorm back at the bunkhouse. Cue a social disaster: I walk over and ask if they mind me joining them. It may well be a language issue, but they are non-committal and clearly embarrassed, so I retreat from the scene with apologies and that feeling of deep discomfort associated with having been found socially wanting.

All is not lost. A couple whom I'd met up at the hut and who'd been keen to meet up for a beer in Saas Grund, are sitting outside one of the other bars. Bracing myself for a second rejection, I ask if I may join them. The answer is – wait for it – yes! Chris and Jo prove lovely company. They are camping up the valley and have come into town for the evening, to celebrate escaping from the clutches of the dreaded Portjenhorn (of 'most evil-looking buttresses' fame). It sounds like they had had a grim time on this peak, moving increasingly slowly while the clock sort-of sped up. I leave the bar feeling a whole lot better.

I am in bed when my unsociable companions return. Like so many before me, I feign to be asleep. And soon I really am.

Monday 9ᵗʰ August

Saas Grund: hiking to Monte Moro Pass

Welcome to the 8:15 early post bus to Mattmark Barrage! It is full. I get a seat, thankfully, and watch with fascination as the guy sat in front of me shows his companion the various and wonderful functions on his wrist watch. To my side, leaning over because of the bodily crush, is a rather nice looking girl (Dutch, I find out later) who is also amused by the spectacle. I catch her eye, try to mime my using the wrist watch to launch the space shuttle, and receive a giggly smile in return. A job well done!

The overburdened bus toils up the long zig-zags to the barrage. With careless familiarity, the driver stops at the top and reverses into the allocated parking space. I glance over my shoulder, see the ever-nearing drop up which we've just climbed, and think back to the final scene in the film *The Italian Job* where the weight of gold stashed on the coach causes it to rock gently over the void. The weight here is bodies, not bullion. Thankfully there is no need for Michael Caine to 'have an idea'. We all just step off the bus, sniff around the car park, and then head up the tarmac to the top of the barrage. I say 'we' because everyone is heading to the lakeside track that leads to the far end of the lake and ultimately to the stony Monte Moro Pass.

The Monte Moro Pass is a walker's link between the (Swiss) Saas valley and the (Italian) Val d'Anzasca with its resort of Macugnaga sitting at the foot of the mighty east face of Monte Rosa. Walkers following the pass are rewarded with a stupendous view of this face and I have always wanted to give it a go. So I have got up early (again!), rushed around the supermarket (again!!) and boarded the 8:15 bus (again!!!).

But that is all behind me – it is breakfast time. I sit cross-legged on the thin grass verge between the track and the lake, eating my yoghurt and feeling smug (in a Tom Sawyer-ish sort of way) as other Monte Moro aspirants pass by and comment on my hunched form. The view across the lake is excellent, with the vivid Rockies-style green of the water backed by striking, individual peaks including the Stellihorn, a mountain I long to climb.

With my food eaten, I take to the track (more a road really) and catch up with the other teams from the bus. It becomes clear that my Dutch friend is part of a large youth group who are also Monte-Moro bound. The track passes through a dark, dripping tunnel reminiscent of the (now inaccessible) Beddgelert tunnels by the Pass of Aberglaslyn in North Wales. I chat with an elderly English couple who are unsure whether they'll make it to the pass; we promise to look out for each other, and then I stride away towards the head of the lake, still half a mile distant. The Dutch party stop to regroup at the head of the lake. I push on, driven by real enthusiasm for the surroundings, the promise of new ground, and the strangers with whom I am sharing this day.

The boulder-strewn path climbs alongside a stream, up a grassy valley peppered with stones. There are lots of us weaving our way upwards, with me being one of the slower ones. For the second time this day, I am reminded forcibly of North Wales: this time of the track from Llyn

Bochlwyd up to the bwlch (saddle) between Tryfan and Glyder Fach. I've spent a lot of my life either visiting or living in North Wales, and its discomforting mix of rugged beauty and industrial archaeology is massively attractive to me. So with such thoughts, I play the silent feet game, concentrating on placing each foot to cause the minimum disruption and noise, which in turn helps me to move well up the hillside. Others have their own ways to 'cope with the slope'. One guy, far fitter than me, races up the hill in short, athletic bursts, only to stop dead on some commanding hillock, to admire the view and presumably to await his less frisky companions. Let's call him Mr Spurt because just now I think he's a tosser.

I find myself in a large punch bowl: flattish, grassy, surrounded by majestic grey peaks, very 'eastern Switzerland' and utterly beautiful. It is a good time to stop, to have some food and drink, and to collect myself for the challenging thousand-foot climb ahead to the crest. Just visible on the skyline is a bronze statue marking the top of the pass. The way to it looks interesting: a curving climb to gain the top of the crags overlooking the punch-bowl where I'm now sat, and then a clamber up sloping rock ramps to the pass.

Having got going again, I climb up the track and over a succession of snow patches, white in the centre but darkened at the edges where the snow butts against boulders. Then, with real curiosity, I start on the sloping rock ramps. They are weird but fascinating underfoot. The rock is laid out like beached whales, with stony gutters in between; not steep but without any semblance of vegetation. I reach a painted marker on a rock (the standard alpine design of two red lines separated by a white line; the whole looking rather like a Liquorice Allsort) and look ahead to see where I must go next. The pattern thus far has been gutter/whale-back/gutter/whale-back, and I am now in a gutter, so... sure enough, I spot the next marker beckoning me to quit the gutter for the next whale-back. I climb up to reach its spine and then walk straight up it with flat feet, sensing through my boots sufficient friction to do this with safety.

Gradually, this ordered regime breaks down into a confusion of large boulders. But it is fun. I see the bronze statue near at hand and with renewed vigour clamber up the final slabs and short chimneys to the top of the pass. Best of all is the final chimney. As I heave myself up it, I notice the Monte Rosa out of the corner of my eye. I register with almost complete detachment that it looks superb.

A minute later, I am standing astride one of the huge boilerplate slabs that make up the summit of the pass, breathing hard, nursing a cold wet back sodden with sweat, and looking with genuine astonishment at the scene before me. Beneath is cloud, a lumpy mass of greyish white hiding the Italian resort of Macugnaga far below. This is no great disappointment, however, because the cloud sea forms a perfect medium out of which sprouts the stupendous east face of Monte Rosa. Its snows may be dirty, its rocks may pelt suitors with casual cruelty, its Marinelli Couloir may be a vicious swine, and its top is definitely capped with grey, angry clouds; but the mountain is stunning and takes my gasping breath away. Directly across the (hidden) valley, there are a chain of lesser peaks which take root at the Monte Rosa and then fade in height until they ultimately drown in the sea of cloud. Behind me, the way I have just come up from Switzerland, the cloud is dark and forbidding and I expect to be rained on before long.

After dealing with the aesthetics, I turn to the mundane: food, drink, warmth and photographs. I also try to resolve a rather strange happening. The bronze statue I saw during the ascent is a full-blown Madonna. Today, many people are clustered about it in some form of ceremony. I hear the unnatural sounds of a PA system and listen aghast as the assembled mass burst into song. I don't know if this is a loved one's funeral or a more general gathering to celebrate or pay remembrance. I sit on a smoothed grey slab and absorb the cocktail of visual and spiritual riches, and take some of the best photographs of the trip. (Please let me share this aside with you. As I type this, many months later, I'm disturbed by the sound of a PA system emanating from the nearby primary school. Isn't that coincidental?)

As I get up to leave, I notice Mr Spurt and his pals on one of the nearby rocks. Our eyes meet – recognition and a smile from him. He is obviously not a bad chap after all and I smile back. To my great pleasure, the English couple from the Mattmark barrage appear amidst the stones. We pass and I hear myself say something horribly patronising about how great it is that they have made it… and then apologise before departing down the now-slippery rocks.

The rain has now set in and this reduces the coefficient of friction on the whale-backs up which I'd climbed so confidently an hour before. This, coupled with aching knees, make the top section of the descent a bit trying. But soon I am skidding across the snow patches with my cagoule opened up (the rain having died down) and a large syringe-full of happiness coursing through my veins. It is good, dammed good. I try to fit the features into scenes from North Wales: the path below the cliff face, leading down to the gorgeous punch bowl, is to be the Devil's Kitchen track leading down from Llyn y Cwn to the base of the Kitchen cleft. I pick my way down it, reaching the welcoming grass of the punch bowl where I stop to absorb the surroundings.

Now I am reminded of the scenery around Arosa in eastern Switzerland (the subject of my reminiscences on Swiss National Day). The town hired, and paid for, mountain guides who took parties up some of the peaks surrounding the resort. We made regular use of this facility: it meant that my dad could share with us the pleasure of the hills without the stress or responsibility of leadership. During our last visit in 1979, I joined these guided parties as a solo climber and relished the experience. One of the other party members took photos. Later, we met in the street in Arosa and he gave me some pictures that included me, which I've kept to this day. I look very young and earnest.

More rain stops these daydreams. I grab my gear, do up my cagoule (and start sweating in the process) and wander down the bouldery track to the lakeside. On reaching it, I opt to walk along the other shore from the morning's wanderings. I race-walk, thrilled by the speed I can reach on this track, looking up every so often to check out the forbidding, rain-sodden crags of the Strahlhorn and

Allalinhorn towering across the lake. The bad light somehow emphasises the banding in their rocks. I recall from my previous visit here in 1989 that at one point, the path bridges a river that falls beneath into the lake's green waters. Here it is! Picture time: the river, the lake, a luckily positioned tree; all help to create a beautiful scene and I snap away with glee. Meanwhile, two walkers who I steamed past earlier now approach and so, with reckless childishness, I quickly pack up and resume my speed walk before they catch up. The end game is the crossing of the barrage to reach the car park the other side.

After a drink, I board the post bus back to Saas Grund. Sitting up front is a guy who insists on sharing with us his party-piece: a vocal imitation of the post bus's horn that the driver sounds at every hair-pin bend. Free entertainment! Eyes meet. Intermittent giggles and titters turn into widespread mirth behind this bloke's back, and the last hair-pin passes to the regret of all, except perhaps the long-suffering driver.

And so passes one of the best day's walking of the trip. This evening, as I sit reading on the balcony, an advance guard from a large team of German climbers enter the dorm. They are lovely and friendly. Amongst them is a lady who subsequently joins me on the balcony, where we pass some time chatting about things. To reach the balcony, one must climb over a cat's cradle of washing lines. Everyone's washing – mine included – is draped over these lines, plus the seat backs and the balcony itself: socks, underpants, partly-soiled hankies, bras, knickers…the works. As we chat, two guys on the tennis court below bash an increasingly sodden tennis ball over a drab net.

I go out to get food. On my return, the German team's ranks have swelled to their full complement, with the new additions as friendly as the advance guard. I am even invited out to dinner, an offer which I decline with thanks. Instead I read, retire to bed, and nurse my still-ticklish cough so that I don't keep everyone awake. What a cracking day.

Tuesday 10th August

Saas Grund: Trip to Hohsaas and Saas Fee

The day starts brightly with an invite to breakfast from my room mates. This is a real treat. They've sussed out that the hotel across the way offers cheap 'all you can eat' breakfasts for impoverished travellers like us. Food and its consumption being a common language, there are no sticky silences around our table as we tackle bread, cheese, jam, hot chocolate and coffee. I enjoy both the food and the company (it was the kindest of gestures to invite along a virtual stranger).

After this feast, we go our separate ways. My friends want to go climbing; I want to realise a long-held dream and take the cable car up to Hohsaas on the slopes of the Weissmies. The weather is gorgeous but I am conscious that on most days during this trip, it deteriorates as the day wears on. So I quickly grab my gear and head for the cable car station just down the road (and fail to tell the lady at the bunkhouse my plans, causing her worry – yet more kindness!). My expectations centre round the much-celebrated view of the Mischabel across the valley, and the keen pleasure of travelling in cable cars. I am not disappointed on either score.

The cable car first climbs to a midway point called Kreuzboden, a beautiful spot with all the usual trimmings (a lake with a cracking view, a café, wooden signposts and a backdrop of mighty peaks), plus in this instance that most British of icons, an old-fashioned red telephone box. I've seen these before in Switzerland, in the towns, but to have one up here seems rather bizarre. I resolve to take pictures of it on my return.

On quitting Kreuzboden, the cable car passes over a sloping desert of stones, up and up, through the magical 3000 metre barrier (the typical headache level for the unaclimatized), to the top of a spur abutting the Weissmies. The view is stunning. Amazingly, after all this time, after all my walking, I still feel spaced out with the altitude when I walk out of the cable car station, a consequence of being whisked up here so fast.

I wander to and fro in the unnatural stillness of the thin air, checking out the best views and taking photographs. It is impossible to take bad pictures; the view is too good for that. Opposite me stands the mighty ridge of peaks collectively called the Mischabel, topped by the Dom and Taschhorn, looking very similar to their aspect from the Almageller Hut a few days before. But there is a slight but significant difference (and I'm now struggling for the right words to convey my thoughts): this new perch, perhaps 5 miles to the north of the Almageller Hut, catches these peaks at an angle rather than straight-on, and in consequence the powerful supporting ridges have greater emphasis. I think this adds to the quality of the scene. There is one big downer, a common problem for mountain photographers working near to alpine cable car stations: I have to work hard to eliminate the trash in the foreground (in this case, coils of wire and fragments of concrete). I want the summits as near to the top of the picture as possible, which entails pointing the camera downward, so catching this trash in the viewfinder. An increasingly impatient search eventually finds a good spot and I snap my shots.

I fancy walking along the track towards the Weissmies towering behind me as it promises a fine view of the glacier. This track is a weird and functional thoroughfare: an undulating stone walkway with wire on the downhill slope, presumably designed for skiers. At its end are climbers removing ropes and crampons having returned from the summit of the Weissmies. I stand by and watch as people untie themselves from their companions, undo crampon straps, pull off helmets (and in some cases, bandannas) and swig water through smiling, chapped lips. The whole alpine climbing 'thing' floods back to me. I confess that on the whole, my pleasure of it has always been retrospective. On the way up the peaks, I was gripped by thoughts of fitness and competence; at the top I was gripped by the exposure and thoughts of the descent; and on the descent, I was gripped by thoughts of softened snow bridges over crevasses and the climber's universal nightmare of rugby-tackling oneself by tripping on one's crampons. So I now feel that I'm a spectator looking at myself from years ago, ridding my body of ropes, harness, crampons and all that alpinism paraphernalia. Now here's a strange thing: I feel an intense guilt standing here watching; not the guilt of a voyeur, but that of someone who turns back partway and is now reunited with those companions who carried on. I fight (and thankfully repress) a strong urge to speak to some of the teams, to let them know that I am one of them, a bona-fide mountain man, and not just a cable car rider.

Back at the cable car station I wander over to the other side and look down the wasteland of stones that leads back to Kreuzboden far below. It really is bleak. By now the weather is turning as I predicted, so after spending a while longer picking out specks of people on the slopes of the Weissmies, I head back down, first to Kreuzboden (stopping there for a picture of the phone box) and thence to Saas Grund.

I travel by bus to Saas Fee and spend the afternoon mooching around its haunts. I don't like it, an amazing statement after the fantastic week that I'd spent there in 1989. Its situation is faultless, on a natural balcony surrounded on three sides by glacier-clad peaks, but its aura fails to impress. An afternoon of admin follows, checking my email, buying film, sorting my bus ticket down to the Rhone valley for the next day (I was off to Zinal), and finding accommodation for my stay in Zinal. This last task is a classic. I won't burden you with the fine detail, but suffice to say that I needed to stay one night in a hotel in Zinal before being able to take up more permanent residence at a recommended bunkhouse. So ensues a laboured conversation with a mercifully patient hotel proprietor, made all the more difficult by my not remembering, in my panic, the French words for either 'tomorrow' or 'Wednesday'. I eventually get my message through and curse my poor grasp of foreign languages. After this exertion, I need a coffee and so drop into a nearby café – to run straight into my first set of room-mates from Saas Grund (of 'can I join you for dinner... no answer' fame). We recognise each other and swap tales of our activities over the last few days. They've been doing yet more of the nearby 4000 metre peaks.

With a lighter heart, I catch the bus back down to Saas Grund, shop for tea and for breakfast the next morning, and spend a quiet evening sorting out my gear, wandering around the town and writing up the diary.

Wednesday 11th August

Journey to Zinal

Today I travel to Zinal. I'm really looking forward to this part of my trip because Zinal is gorgeous and I have big plans for myself while there. So I board the bus to Brig in good spirits and peer out of the window as we speed through avalanche galleries and past village after village on our descent back to the Rhone valley. Yet again, I am bound for Brig railway station. Once there, I buy a ticket to Sierre (my next port of call, westwards down the Rhone valley, heading back towards Lake Geneva), wander lazily to the board showing the train times, absorb its contents and realize that at a fast waddle (I'm heavily laden) I can just make the next train... and I do. At Sierre, I suss out where to get the bus up to Zinal and then act on a plan designed to make life easier for me, namely to dump as much surplus gear as possible in a railway locker and carry only one bag with me up to Zinal. And then it is time for food.

Cut to the most dangerous part of the trip. After eating a lovely lunch, I decide to walk into Sierre town centre to pass the time before the next Zinal bus. The wander around is fine. However, on crossing the road to return to the railway station (the departure point for the Zinal bus), I make eye contact with some drunken guy who is crossing the other way. He looks, I shrug, and then he starts mouthing off at me… 'blah, blah un problem?' which I loosely interpret as 'have you got a problem with me, because I fancy kicking your 'effing head in'. I walk on stoutly, ignoring his shouts wafting across the street as best I can while dreading the sound of approaching footsteps from behind. But thankfully it is all hot air. From the shadows of the railway station, I watch him totter up the street into town, colliding into a shop window on his way.

It's a male thing, I guess, or maybe it's just me, but fear turns first to anger and then to rage. I've been made to look a fool and have walked away from a fight (or that's how I feel). I literally clench my teeth with seething rage as I wait anxiously for the arrival of the bus and, God-forbid, Mr 'Un Problem'. He never shows.

The bus is very busy. I am still really out of sorts (as I write this, it all seems so dreadfully silly) and make a most discomforting companion for my neighbour sitting next to me. When we eventually talk to each other, I realize with both horror and shame that my episode of teeth-clenching rage has tired out the jaw muscles necessary for coherent speech.

Zinal stands at the end of the Val d'Anniviers, which like the Zermatt and Saas valleys thrusts southwards from the Rhone valley, into the mountains. In its lower reaches, the valley is seriously dramatic. The road is no less so: it hugs the cliff-side in desperation and I find myself praying that no traffic will come along in the other direction. Passengers on the drop side (of which I am one) are treated to a gripping view over the inadequate retaining wall, down the cliff face to the river far, far below. It should not have been a surprise for me: I've been to Zinal twice before; once on my own, on the bus as now; and once with my brother and his wife in their over-laden but gutsy Mini. The valley opens out in its higher reaches. You pass through a beautiful picture-postcard village called Vissoie. The valley head, where Zinal sits, has a very open aspect.

I get off the bus in a calmer frame of mind than when I embarked and do a quick walk around the centre, mainly to remind myself where everything is. Little has changed: the Post Office, Guides Bureau, the restaurant that served the most memorable meal I've ever had, they are all here. Also the mountains are as I remembered. The valley-head beyond the village is a sort-of plain, blocked at its top by the Grand Cornier, Dent Blanche, Pointe du Zinal and the Besso, in a manner very reminiscent of Mickleden at the head of Great Langdale, with Zinal being Stool End farm. The Besso is closest, a tall rock peak almost Dolomitic in character; a poor man's Machapuchare (a Himalayan peak above Pokhara), with a snake's forked tongue for a summit.

The sides of the valley are made up of wooded, craggy slopes, hiding on the east side the beautiful summit of the Weisshorn and her companions. Do you recognise these names? The Zinal valley abuts, and is west of, the Zermatt valley and it co-owns, with Zermatt, the dividing ridge which contains the Weisshorn, the Dent Blanche and all their courtiers.

However, in character, Zinal is a thousand miles from Zermatt. For a start, it is exclusively French-speaking. But crucially, it is small and not over-developed and you really do get a feeling of being up amidst the peaks. I love it and will go back again, for a fourth time.

I find the hotel where I am staying for this one night. It's a bit rough round the edges, but the warmth and friendliness of the owner more than makes up for this. She is lovely. She speaks no English, and I pitifully little French, so our interactions are perforce very expressive. Essential communications are achieved and I find myself sitting in the bar downstairs, sipping a glass of wine that she has recommended, having dumped my trash in my room (it is a novel event having sleeping quarters to myself).

In the evening, I go out to shop for food for the next day and search for the Hotel Alpina, where I have booked bunkhouse accommodation for the remainder of my stay in Zinal. I eventually find it at the top of the village, the last residence before the plain at the head of the valley. It will prove to be the happiest of places to stay. But for now, I return to the hotel, phone the Grand Mountet Hut to book a bed four nights hence, wash myself and my clothes, and retire to a proper bed (wow!) for an early start.

Thursday 12ᵗʰ August

Zinal: climbing the Corne de Sorebois

This is certainly a different sort of climb! Instead of being overtaken by the usual gang of fit hill-goers, I have just made way for a guy driving a Peugeot and now watch aghast and deflated as he pulls away up the bumpy track, leaving me in a cloud of dust and burning clutch fumes.

While in Zermatt, you may recall, I'd managed to borrow a more recent copy of my guidebook (thirty years more recent, in fact) to check out my planned itinerary for the stay in Zinal. It made both depressing and realistic reading. It was clear from its texts that my top choice of peak, the Pigne de La Lé, was a no-go for a solo climber with my skill-set and I needed to look elsewhere for a peak to climb. The answer was the far easier Corne de Sorebois, a recommended summit above Zinal, with good views and low stress levels.

So here I am, walking up the dusty service road to the Sorebois cable car terminus, a route used by construction traffic, punters in French hatch-backs (!) and those hill-goers like me who are too proud and stupid to ask the locals for their advice. To add insult to injury, the weather is closing in and cloud masks my intended peak. But the going is easy and at last I can see the terminus in the distance. It looks a long way off. I pull down the brim of my hat so that I can no longer see how far there is to go, and continue on, cursing as much as my laboured breathing allows. A shepherd passes with two dogs, one of whom appears to be having a 'bad hair' day. The shepherd's screaming and shouting has little effect on the mutt's behaviour; it ranges to-and-fro, either deaf to, or oblivious of, its master's commands. No 'One Man and His Dog' team this!

Half a sweaty hour later, I reach the cable car terminus, dump my sack on an outside chair and walk into what could best be described as a motorway service station. Elton John croons through the building and adds to the growing unreality of the day. I fill up my water bottle and walk back outside to rest and look at the view. It is good, very good. The tops are wreathed in cloud, but the shapes formed by their lower slopes look intriguing and I find myself trying to imagine where the actual summits lie, rather like a 'spot the ball' competition in a newspaper. Eating away, I relax and have a wry giggle at the fortunes of the day. Certainly this is stress-free. Turning round, I see the onwards track snaking into the mist, its course looking every bit as dull as the enveloping vapours.

Now I am cold so I decide to get going. It is alright and I feel a growing sense of pleasure as I move up the inevitable zig-zags and into the mist. I reminisce about a day some years earlier, during my ten-month stay in Australia in which I travelled for a while and then worked as an oceanography demonstrator at ADFA, the Australian Defence Force Academy in Canberra. One bank holiday weekend, I travelled from Canberra to the White Mountains for a walking trip. Queue one of the best weekends of the Australian trip. I stopped at a hostel in the main resort, Thredbo. From there I climbed Mount Kosciusko (Australia's highest peak) in thick mist and then, the next day, the far superior Mount Townsend (Australia's second highest peak) in glorious sunshine. The Kosciusko walk shared much with today, except that there the track from the cable car station was made up largely of metal grills that bounced like a springboard under my sturdy frame.

With all this day-dreaming, I fail to notice that the cloud is breaking up, leaving the summit of the Corne de Sorebois clear. I speed up, hoping beyond hope that the dullness of the climb will be superseded by a beautiful vista. And so it proves! At last I reach the skyline, to be punched in the face by a stunning sight: the deep, glacial green of the Lac du Grimentz, backed by the jumble of peaks separating Zinal from the distant French resort of Chamonix. Not all is clear. Mont Blanc, reputedly visible from here, is a no-show and I also cannot make out the bold Himalayan pyramid of the Grand Combin (an alpine version of the Himalayan peak Dhaulagiri, methinks). I pick my way up the short ridge to the summit.

The top of the Corne de Sorebois is a smooth dome of grass supported by pastoral slopes that drop away to give emphasis to the beautiful view. Straight ahead, at my feet, is the Val d'Anniviers (the valley up which you travel to reach Zinal), backed by the peaks on the far side of the Rhone valley. There are villages everywhere, clinging to the soft grass slopes, some with churches, some without. Clearly visible on the farther side of the Rhone valley, is an imposing modern building with three tower blocks (in the resort of Crans-Montana, I think). It reminds me forcibly of the Barbican in London and also of the single white tower block on the Anglesey side of the Menai Straits in North Wales, a sight familiar to devotees of northern Snowdonia. Turning to the right, I can see over Zinal (itself hidden) to the supporting slopes of the Weisshorn and Zinal Rothorn. The peaks themselves, sadly, are still lost in cloud, but I have a sense of expectancy that they will clear. I turn around to look back along the summit ridge, the last bit of which I've just climbed: it stretches over a succession of impressive peaks to end abruptly at the triangle of the Dent Blanche. Imagine an alpine version of the view from Lose Hill to Mam Tor above Castleton, with its appealing connecting ridge, and you have the idea.

I am not alone. People are milling around the summit, eating or taking pictures or just soaking up the view. Some have sat down on the gentle grass slope falling towards the Lac du Grimentz, perhaps drawn by its vivid turquoise colouring. As I myself sit down, just by the top, another explanation presents itself: the summit is covered in goat/sheep shit. I kick away the little brown balls to expose the grass underneath, and settle down to eat.

At last, the cloud clears fully to reveal the mighty Weisshorn and her neighbours. It is beautiful. The Weisshorn is a long whaleback from here, supported to its right by a succession of sharp, highly individual companions, the chief of which is the Zinal Rothorn. A carefully aimed shell, fired over this peak, would land in Zermatt. In a rare moment of mental clarity, I decide that it is the valleys and ridges radiating downwards from these peaks which make the view so eye-catching. The ridges interlink with each other like tender lovers, leaving just enough space between for a succession of finely sculpted hanging valleys. Photography is a disaster. First-off, the film disconnects from the wind-on (as happened on the Mettelhorn at the start of the trip). This time, I am better prepared and put in a new film. Picture taking then ensues until I suddenly realise that the new film has a different film speed to that of its faithless predecessor. Cursing, I take my pictures a third time!

I wander down the summit cone, past the cattle in the basin beneath, to arrive at the motorway service station. This strikes a discordant note after the joys of the summit view, so after filling up on essential fluids, I take the long, dusty track to Zinal, thinking about my new lodgings for the night and my plans for the next few days.

Hang on! I'm sure this fence wasn't here this morning? There is no mistake – it is a fence, and an electric one at that. Fearing both retribution and electrocution, I meekly obey the exhortation daubed on the flimsy wooden sign ('Zinal') and take to a rutted track heading directly downhill towards the valley. All is well until this disappears amidst a glade of tussocks and cow-shit! I am not impressed. Hot and a little peeved, I carry on down, trying to 'read' the ground to suss out where a Zinal-bound track might go. I do not find it. Instead I stumble across some workmen digging a hole. They kindly point me in the right direction and, sure enough, I soon find myself on a sort of track heading straight down. This is certainly direct, rather like a helter-skelter. It flits through the trees in tight zig-zags, at a steepness that makes my knees scream and sweat pop out of every pore. My main fear (apart from super-heated, melting knee cartilage) is that this will prove to be yet another blind alley and I will be left stranded in these precipitous woods. At one point, I take to my bum to spare my poor old knees; at another, I pass a woman with a youngster, both of whom seem similarly ill-at-ease with the lunatic route. Eventually, the helter-skelter ends and I find myself on a wide and blessedly horizontal woodland track, separated from Zinal only by the river. A bridge appears. I cross it with gratitude, to emerge at the back of the shops.

It is still quite early in the day. I go to the hotel, down a pint of something nice and then reclaim my boxful of gear stashed in the back of the bar. Now for yet another house move. The Hotel Alpina, where I plan to stay for the rest of my time in Zinal, is at the top end of the resort, the last habitation before the big plain that leads into the hills. It is all that I could have asked for: friendly, relaxed and perfect for the lone traveller. An English lady (Nadia) and her Swiss husband run the place. They have two lovely kids and a small, excitable puppy which constantly takes the youngest child's toys for its own, propelling them across the bar floor so that they smash against the walls.

The shared dorm is up a very steep stair, almost a ladder. It is lovely. I take a spot at the end of one of the 'runs' and then do my best to make it home, laying out my blanket and jamming all my gear into one of the nearby wooden lockers. Next I have a shower. As so often happens, I can taste the day's accumulated dirt, salt and suncream as the rivulets of water stream down past my mouth en-route to the plug-hole. My next task is clothes washing. This is easily done, but as ever the drying is a pain. There is a patio above the bar, so I take myself and my sopping wet clothing up to it, to sit on the bench and mentally 'will' everything to dry. My meditation is broken by the sound of a window being opened onto the patio. Out pops a head from which spouts English. The guy (Peter) has also just arrived at the hotel. He and his wife have taken a room, which to his surprise is overlooked by a public-access patio populated by a weirdo drying his washing. We chat amiably for a while.

During the evening I manage to make contact with an old Bangor friend of mine, a French guy called Jerome who now lives and works in Lausanne. We arrange that I can stop with him for a night, on my way across to the Bernese Alps where I am to meet up with friends from Merseyside. So Zinal marks the end of the solo trip, and in truth I am not sorry. But first I have three days in which to do good things and I'm excited.

Friday 13th August

Zinal: hiking to Arpittetaz Hut

Zinal footpaths are fine just so long as you use common sense and a map. Sadly I have brought neither commodity to this cold, dewy morning, which is my explanation for why I am yet again on my bum on a precipitous woodland track above Zinal, this time in retreat. Here's why...

For years, I've wanted to visit the shy and retiring Arpittetaz Hut, snuggling at the foot of the mighty Weisshorn. Today was the day to realise this dream. Unfortunately, after walking across the plain towards the peaks, I'd been enticed up a track sign-posted to the hut without (a) checking the map or (b) the necessary French to translate the message 'Pas de Chasseurs' daubed on the sign-post. The path was very narrow and extremely steep, climbing ever upwards to a band of cliffs through which I could see no obvious route. I was right – there was no obvious route. Suddenly I found myself at the top of a steep muddy slope, above which rose the cliffs. A metal (toilet?) chain dangled out of a dark corner, teasing me to commit myself further; but its upward course was hidden and I sensed that once I grabbed it to start climbing, any back-tracking would be nasty. So with little regret I had turned around and headed back down... on my bum.

Back to the here and now. I cannot waste the day, so the plan is to retrace my steps to the valley plain and rejoin the main trail to the Petit Mountet Hut, a lesser prize than the Arpittetaz Hut.

Things are getting better. The sun is out, the dew is steaming off the vegetation and I have just seen a bird of prey. And wow... I have also just seen the proper path to the Arpittetaz Hut! I check the time... 9am... massively late by alpine hill-walking standards... but I don't care as I desperately want to visit this hut. So I follow the path, first through bushes, to a crossing over a boisterous river, and then up the bank on the far side. This is a joy. The path is covered with small white stones that crunch under my feet. It twists and turns through yet more bushes, in a wild-west setting, before climbing steeply into the forest beyond.

Soon I start to worry a little. The Arpittetaz Hut stands at the head of a side valley and my current path seems to be heading the wrong way. This time I use the map. All is well. The track is simply taking its time, mounting the slopes in long, kindly zig-zags; and sure enough an expected lake, the Lac d'Arpittetaz, appears amidst the rolling landscape. I stop by its shoreline for a bite to eat and to give the wind-ruffled surface a chance to settle and its reflections to re-form. Others are here too, including a couple (plus dog) with whom I will play leapfrog for much of the day.

With genuine anticipation, I take to the path beyond. This leads me up the side valley towards the hut. A pattern emerges: long, leisurely stretches above the valley floor that eat up the distance to the hut, interspersed with short, crumbly zig-zags that eat up the requisite height gain. Regrettably, I can see the hut in the distance, a permanent and unwelcome reminder of how far I need to go. A raging torrent is bridged by a flimsy metal construction that shakes as I stride purposefully across. Beneath me the water hurtles past in a deafening roar, spewing in jets as it forces its way between boulders. I love it and want to stay longer; but instead I carry on, satisfying myself with a self-promise to stop here on my return.

The hut is now nearby, standing at the top of a tongue of hill sandwiched between two streams. I reach the confluence of the streams and begin the weary climb up the dividing tongue. I am tired and just want to get there. I force myself not to look up in case the vision crushes me with disappointment.

I arrive, at last, and what a wonderful place to be! Dumping my sack by one of the outside benches, I take a much-needed drink of water and then rummage for my jumper. My sweaty shirt comes off to be replaced by this jumper, making me feel better immediately even though the wool rubs against my skin. The shirt I spread out to dry.

Perhaps it's the tables and benches (she and I often lunched together in Cambridge at a rough-and-ready pub with similar benches, renowned for its Thai food), but as I sit here under the alpine sun with my own unseeing hazel eyes, I think of a pair of green eyes, and of lips that curled upwards to suppress a laugh when told something crude but amusing. She and I were firm friends. It was 'look but don't touch' as she had a boyfriend, but I fell head-over-heels for her and told her so. Amazingly, our friendship survived this disclosure; but what with her improving relationship with her man and my increasing neediness due to loneliness and the rigours of redundancy, the friendship first faltered and then exploded in a fireball of recrimination. Thankfully, we parted as friends when I left both my job and Cambridge to make this trip.

There are four others at the hut: a couple whom I presume to be the hut guardians and two guys who seem on friendly terms with them. They all say hello and I return the courtesy. I wander into the hut to look around. Wood is everywhere – tables and chairs, floor, walls, the lot – and its darkened colouring has great character. This speaks to me of a spiritual retreat and I like what I both see and feel. I move quietly around the room, looking at the pictures and notices pinned to the walls and generally soaking up the atmosphere. One of the hut guardians comes in to serve up a bowl of soup for someone. I ask for one myself, pay up, and take it outside to eat while looking at the view.

With the exception of the ascent path, visibly snaking along the valley side far below, there is not a single sign of human intervention to be seen: no houses, cable car stations, pylons, or driveable tracks – nothing. So I am looking at real alpine wilderness. The valley far below, dead straight, has a river flowing down its base, passing through a wasteland of grass hummocks and stone, and I can trace the river's course until it disappears over a lip on its way to the main Zinal valley. Beyond, the view is blocked off by a wall of cloudy peaks, with tops only slightly higher than the hut. I guess that when clear, one could see much further in this direction. To my left, above the heads of my four companions, stands a superb example of natural art: tiered icefalls spilling over bands of rock like the salt deposits at Mammoth in Yellowstone National Park, but here overtopped by the sharp needle of the Zinal Rothorn.

For me to see the rest of the view, in particular my pal the Weisshorn, I need to shift my butt. I get up and walk behind the hut. The west face of the Weisshorn looks both huge and savage, a gargantuan Snowdon from the Gladstone memorial on the Watkin Track. Whoever designed this mountain did a first class job and many (me included) think it to be the most beautiful peak in the Alps. However, the designer has perhaps blitzed all his/her energies on its ridges and other two faces, for here I am faced with an impressive but somewhat ugly wall, like a spare bedroom awaiting the cash and motivation for a face-lift. The peak itself has a bizarre halo of cloud that catches the sun, giving it the starkness of a photographic negative. In the worsening weather it almost sends shivers down my spine. Before turning away, I remember to pay homage to the Weisshorn's shy and crumbling neighbour, the Schalihorn, with its two summits sticking up like a pair of owl's ears. There are things to see nearer at hand, principally a lovingly arranged wood pile just behind the hut, looking like an opened fir cone. I've never seen wood stacked this way and take far too many photographs of it under the darkening skies.

On my return to the front of the hut, more people have arrived and I can also see some fast movers on their way up from the valley. The lady guardian comes over and we chat about the hut, its ring of peaks and that dreadful path with its toilet chain. She confirms that there is still a demand for the hut, which is music to my ears because the place has such character. The 'toilet chain' path is bad, she confirms. Fit for shit, one might say! Thanks to the language barrier, I am credited with better mountaineering judgement than I deserve. By the way, what is French for 'retreat on buttocks as a consequence of incompetence'?

The weather is definitely worsening so I pack my stuff, say my goodbyes and make my way back down. An increasing roar heralds my arrival at the raging torrent. But a promise is a promise, so I sniff around for a good vantage point, look up at the sky to see if a bright patch is due (it is) and then wait quietly for the sun to smile on the scene. It smiles, I click, and then I resume my downward trek. As I walk, I exchange greetings with a succession of fell runners heading upwards to the hut. From snatched conversation, both now and later on, I gather that these are Mexicans, a sort-of running team or something. I've got a big soft spot for Mexicans, principally because I worked with a gang of them at the School of Ocean Sciences in Menai Bridge and they were great fun. One lunch time, their wives laid on a real Mexican meal and I remember eating and drinking to excess. We did Tequila slammers, I recall.

Such reminiscences help me down the remainder of the path to the Lac d'Arpittetaz. I'm getting quite tired by now and plan to eat something to provide the necessary drive to reach Zinal, still a long way off. The lakeside is busy. I pick out Spanish from the babble of voices and this adds weight to my Mexican fell runner theory. There are English-speaking voices too. One such belongs to an American lady living in Montreux. She is out with friends and some kids. We amble down together, chatting amiably. By chance, she is friends with the couple who run the Hotel Alpina where I am staying. Now I am alone again, wandering through the thinning woods, along a mercifully soft track, and then across the large plain back to Zinal and the welcome haven of 'home'.

After the familiar afternoon rituals of showering, shopping, laundry and reading, I hook up with Eckardt, a fascinating German guy who is also staying at the Hotel Alpina. I thought that he had an Irish accent when I first heard him and was consequently amazed to learn that he was German (he plays in an orchestra in Mannheim, mid-Germany). He, I, and Peter and his wife Claire take dinner together in the Hotel Alpina and have a good giggle (mostly at Scousers' expense, which means me). Happy times!

Saturday 14ᵗʰ August

Zinal: hiking to Grand Mountet Hut for overnight stay

I think that of all the places on this trip where I've sat and rested, this has to be the most beautiful. It is truly amazing and quite different.

I am sat on the lip of a grassy ledge, perhaps 20 metres wide, which carries the path to the Grand Mountet Hut. It is still early and the stark cliffs of the Besso, behind my back, cast a shadow over the valley. But here is the weirdest of things: if I peer down the tumbling slopes, I can see the shadow of the Besso's twin-forked, snake-tongue summit etched out on the ice of the Zinal Glacier far below, a wonderful sight indeed. The slopes on the other side of the glacier are bathed in sun: dangerous, crumbling cliffs lead my eye to the Petit Mountet Hut, sited somewhat below my level. A large party issues from this hut as I sit watching. They start to climb a zig-zag track up the hillside behind. To my left, also in sunlight, stand the Dent Blanche and its smaller but similarly shaped neighbour, the Grande Cornier. Both peaks are triangles from this angle and I see in them an uncanny resemblance to the Pyramids in Egypt.

Obviously the cold is getting to my wits! For the first time on this trip, I put on my bobble hat. I also eat some chocolate as I sense tough times ahead. I am right. The grassy ledge thins out as it climbs towards a prominent spur. I stop briefly here (on the spur) and absorb with little pleasure the way ahead: a climbing traverse across a loose, steep, grey, cold and unwelcoming face, literally stinking with the sulphurous menace of stonefall.

First I need to cross a sort of chute or gutter that issues like a sewer drain from the cliffs towering above. Such is the volume of stonefall down this chute that the path's engineers have constructed a wooden gallery through which the path creeps. Fallen rocks smother the gallery roof; presumably new arrivals must find space by displacing some of the current incumbents to the glacier far below. I take a deep breath, grab the iron chain protecting the path at this point, and head down the side as fast as I dare, into the gallery with its dripping water, and up the other side, stopping only when I feel safe.

So far, so good. Now the path climbs in zig-zags up the face, working rightwards, aiming for a high point on a far spur. Again the engineers have been at work, installing yet more metal cable to serve as a handrail, so I put on my gloves to protect my hands and then grab the cable as I pick my way along. Two Italians are coming down. Somehow I find the breath to talk and thus discover that the hut is still an hour distant. No matter, I have all day and I am rushing now only because I hate the feel of this face. I am nervous. To help overcome this, I try one of my old tricks: imagining that I'm guiding someone who is reliant on me. I talk to this person in my head and for some reason this helps. Finally, with a last crossing to the right, I stand on yet another spur, but this time with the face now behind me. I look back and realise with genuine anguish that I must pass this way again on the morrow.

The spur is a gateway to a brighter world. I am out of the cold shadows and ready to enter the vast basin created by the circuit of peaks from the Besso, over the Zinal Rothorn and Obergabelhorn, to the mighty Dent Blanche. But I am not yet at the hut and between me and it lies a sea of boulders over which I must totter to reach journey's end.

With renewed vigour, I follow the usual painted markers, finding the best footing through the rockery. Stone rests on stone. I tap a precarious looking one with my boot before committing my full body weight to it. The received sound tells me it is secure. Sometimes, I gradually gain speed, only to realise that I'm moving too quickly to make sensible foot placements. Then I slow down, lose balance and with it confidence, and curse freely as I wobble from edge to edge. However, the game is good and in a short while I see the hut near to hand, backed by the searing white of its surrounding peaks. I have waited literally years to see this sight. It is a strange and somehow unreal sensation, not unlike seeing a loved pop band in the flesh after years of fan-worship. With these feelings I walk the final metres to the hallowed Grand Mountet Hut.

The building is the usual two-storey stone structure with brightly painted window shutters. It also has the weirdest toilet block in the world, which seems to overhang the slopes below and is reached down a set of iron steps.

The well-known view is as utterly unique as a fingerprint and perhaps one of the best I've ever seen. Imagine if you will a huge, poorly drawn semicircle of peaks, centred at the Grand Mountet Hut and with a radius varying from two to five miles (hardly a rigorous mathematical description). Glaciers feed from these perimeter peaks to converge into a vast ice traffic jam that passes before the hut. As I look out from the hut courtyard to the perimeter peaks, I see to my left the sharp, blatant Zinal Rothorn, partly masked by the intervening slopes behind the hut, with next, to its right, the small delicate cone of the Trifthorn and then the elegant Obergabelhorn, a much-photographed sight from here. Now follows the distant but no less impressive pair of the Mont Durand and the Pointe du Zinal, between which lies the Col Durand, a relatively mellow crossing point to Zermatt via the Schonbuhl Hut. Straight ahead, towering over me despite being across the glacier, are the mighty Dent Blanche and the Grand Cornier. The Dent Blanche wins the 'X Factor' prize: a stunning pyramid with simple, graceful lines that stand out even in this crowd of beauties. Behind the hut lie arid, stony slopes which block off the view to the peaks in that direction.

I perform my now-familiar ablutions in the weirdo toilet block. Whoever drew the male/female signs to designate the genders had a great sense of humour! I giggle despite the numbness from the ice-cold water spreading up from my extremities. Then I drink and eat while sitting and admiring the view. It's still relatively early (11-ish) and the place is quiet apart from a man-and-boy team preparing to head back down to Zinal.

Early afternoon, I go for a walk up the usual 'onwards' path from the hut – the one taken by alpinists in the early hours. This leads me along to the foot of a moraine ridge, which I then start to climb in the hope of expanding my horizons (!) and perhaps unblocking the view of the hidden peaks behind the hut. I go as far as I am comfortable. From here onwards, the path deteriorates into an ankle-snapping boulder field. I search for a stone seat with a shape that promises comfort for my behind (there are few contenders, I fear). Now suitably ensconced, I take in the view, a very decent upgrade of that seen from the hut. All of a sudden I hear the distant fall of stones. I can't immediately locate its source, so I scan the huge semi-circle of peaks in earnest, spotting at last a rising column of smoke in one of the rocky gullies of the Grand Cornier. To my amazement, the stone-fall is still going on and I watch with awe as a stone perhaps the size of a car (I exaggerate not) bounces down the face in lengthening leaps, wreaking havoc in its wake. Sulphur smells soon fill the air. Finally the dust settles and everything returns to normal as if nothing has happened, rather like the aftermath of a kill on the African plains. I remain long at this perch, taking pictures and scrutinizing the lovely scene. But as so often happens, the advancing afternoon brings worsening weather and with it a build-up of clouds that denies me of the sun's warmth.

People are now arriving at the hut. One group (three guys from Belgium) I know from the Hotel Alpina. Later on, they kindly invite me to sit with them at dinner, a lovely gesture. I am fascinated by the antics of a large trekking party, also from Belgium it seems. Finally a family arrive in the now-poor weather: mum, dad and two kids, the youngest being perhaps seven years old and justly proud of having reached the hut (I am well impressed). My limited German is sufficient to decipher the words 'stone-fall' and 'ibex' from their tale; but with this nosey eavesdropping comes a just reward: the cold stab of fear as I contemplate my passage of 'the gutter' and its environs tomorrow morning.

Dinner is fun. The chicken curry is excellent and I gladly accept a glass of wine from the Belgian guys. We talk mountains, and then as they return to chatting amongst each other, I start to chat with a father-and-son team who are seated nearby. The time passes nicely. Suddenly, as darkness approaches, there is a bustle in the room that reminds me of people awaiting a train, as one person and then another see evidence of the train's imminent arrival. However the arrival is not that of the 8:15 to Crewe, but a clearing in the weather. I grab what warmth I have to hand and dash outside to join others in the courtyard. The tip of the Dent Blanche sticks up above the thinning clouds, glowing violent purple as it catches the last rays of the sun. It is too dark for a picture; and anyway, it seems uncouth to clutter the moment with technology. We shiver and chatter as the mists clear. I recall it as a most beautiful sight.

Eventually I head back in. One of the Belgian guys stops to chatter. As far as I can tell, he and his friends are geographers (town planners?) working for the government but who are destined to lose their jobs because of a change in the party in power. I suspect I'm missing the fine detail that would help strengthen the tale. But he's a fun guy and his English is a damned sight better than my Flemish. Gratefully I head to my dorm and bed down for the night. Perhaps it is the over-hot duvet, or the powerful happenings of the day, but sleep eludes me for a long while, and its final arrival heralds some very odd dreams.

Sunday 15th August

Zinal: return from Grand Mountet Hut and quiet afternoon

It's 5:45 in the morning and I'm up and about, standing and watching in the courtyard as dawn strikes hard, turning the snows from a cold bluish grey to a dazzling incandescent white. My camera is busy taking pictures of the Dent Blanche. Meanwhile, my fingers freeze in the cold, so between shots I warm them up by blowing on them and, when no-one is looking, stuffing them down my crutch (drastic, perhaps even illegal in public, but effective). The climbing teams left the hut some hours earlier. One group I can still see far off: four tiny dots making their way across the vast glacier basin to the Col Durand, presumably en-route to Zermatt.

Breakfast is the usual bread and jam with a huge mug of cocoa for extras, taken in the company of my new-found Belgian friends. A lovely morning in all respects.

That was about an hour ago. I now stand at the top of the spur overlooking the shadowy, intimidating slope which I must now cross to reach the lower but equivalent spur on its far side. I tighten the belt on my sack (good protection for the neck and back in the event of a fall) and start to pick my way along the track. A steeper section is reached. I grab the cold metal cable serving as a handrail, only to realise that I haven't put on my gloves to give my hands protection from the lacerating cable. As I stop, a stone perhaps the size of a tennis ball falls from just above the path, to bounce in front of me and then speed its way to the glacier far below. This has the impact of an atomic bomb! I need to up my game. So I stride out as fast as is safe, reach the drop into the now-legendary gutter, and whisk my way down and across into the shelter of the roofed gallery, my right hand running along the handrail as a safety precaution. A deep breath for the climb out... up, up and out of the shade, out of the gutter, onto the sun-dappled spur and its assurance of safety. Phew... I didn't like that.

I am not alone. As I sit on the spur, chilling out and nibbling chocolate after the mad-dash crossing that I'd just made, I notice that the large Belgian trekking party from the hut are now crossing the slope. I sense a photo opportunity: the team in a long colourful line following the path into the gutter, in the manner of porters on a Himalayan expedition. With a calmness and order that relegates my mad-dash to the annals of incompetence, they walk around a corner and, without breaking step, drop down the path, pass through the covered walkway and climb up to my stance. Here they stop. We swap pleasantries. They're on an organised tour. I ask about their itinerary and am amazed to discover that it is both real and exciting: a multi-day trek around the head of the Zinal valley, interspersed with visits to the valley to replenish supplies. I have a flash of inspiration: here is the party I saw quitting the Petit Mountet Hut the morning before. Today they head down to replenish, only then to climb back out of the valley to yet another hut, the Cabane du Tracuit (at 3200 metres, one of the higher of the alpine huts and well worth a visit).

In 1986, I came to the Alps to take pictures and go walking. The first big thing I did was visit the Cabane du Tracuit. It was a tough day as I was not yet acclimatized. Anyway, on arrival there, I decided to cheer myself up with a nice bottle of beer. Big mistake! Five minutes later, I was 'picking my spot' outside the back of the hut, readying myself to be sick. Suffice to say that I felt bloody miserable and retreated to bed early. Thankfully this stupidity did not last. Song and laughter drifted up from downstairs. I squashed all thoughts of self-pity and headed back to the throng and a great evening. It was intensely cold the next morning, but this was a small price to pay for the staggering scene. I got my pictures that fine morning, the best of which was a poignant shot of my footprints in the snow, issuing from the hut door as I headed for the valley.

So back to the current trip. I wax lyrical about the Cabane du Tracuit, then realise that I sound like a boring old fart telling folk stuff they already know. We head off down the path at the same time, so consequently I become intermingled with the group, a real treat for me as they are talkative and friendly. Sadly, this spell of companionship ends all too soon: we reach the bridge at the valley head under the mid-morning sun and take our parting; they to stock up with supplies and rest awhile before the big climb; me to take the now-familiar track out of the woods and across the grassy plain to Zinal.

I feel a mix of emotions, mainly reflective. The 'big-walking' part of the trip is now over. It got off to a poor start with being ill; and though Zermatt was fun, I accept that I did not make best use of my time while there. However, the last week or so, spent in Saas Grund and here in Zinal, had been fantastic, more than I could have wished for. The remainder of the trip would have a different focus, namely meeting up with friends and doing some sight-seeing.

My reverie is broken by the strangest of sights. A football match is being held on the grassy plain and some spectators have driven their cars along the gravel track from Zinal to the makeshift pitch. A few cows are moving between the parked cars, looking like thieves having a furtive foray in the hunt for an ill-secured vehicle. The sight makes me laugh and lifts my melancholy mood.

Monday 16ᵗʰ August

Zinal: hiking to Petit Mountet Hut

Today the only cash-point in Zinal has broken down, disrupting my plans to take the bus to a small village called Chandolin, high up above the Val d'Anniviers.

Everyone flusters around the cash-point, asking the poor staff at the nearby tourist information bureau when it is likely to be fixed. Phone calls ensue and an answer provided... some time today. I am less bothered than many: I'll go for a walk this morning and if on my return Zinal is still financially dry, I'll head down to the next town in the valley (Vissoie) to scour for cash outlets there.

So off I head to the hills yet again, this time to the Petit Mountet Hut on the side of the Glacier du Zinal. The hut is at a relatively low altitude (2400 metres) and is a low-key objective. I was there in 1986. My way goes first across the now-familiar plain, then by some tracks through the woods at its head, and finally up the edge of a steep spine of moraine to the cheery hut. It is a lovely walk, full of interest. However, the woods are also full of buzzing flies and I worry that my heavy indrawn breaths will swallow some of them in the manner of a whale grazing on krill.

I reach the hut having avoided swallowing any flies. Outside are the usual tables and benches so I settle down to eat and admire the gorgeous view, dominated by the precipices of the Besso on the other side of the glacier. I pick out, on its lower slopes, the path to the Grand Mountet Hut. After a while I head inside to look around. It is most welcoming, looking like it has been done out fairly recently. I have confirmation that this is so: there are picture boards on the wall, rather like those you see in pubs (plastered with photos of the regular drinkers), showing scenes of people working on a refit of the hut. It all reminds me of the pictures in Pete's Eats in Llanberis.

In times gone by, the route to the Grand Mountet Hut was on this side of the Glacier du Zinal, passing by the Petit Mountet Hut before heading on to the glacier. This was my reason for visiting the hut back in 1986. So, out of curiosity, I seek out the old onward path as it marches precariously along the knife-edge crest of crumbling moraine. It looks no better now than it did in 1986.

Back in Zinal, the cash-point is now working. Replenished with cash, I splash out on a newspaper and a coffee and take up residence at a table outside one of the hotels. However, the sky grows steadily more threatening and eventually spots of rain start to splatter on the newspaper, a noise both entertaining and disappointing. So I revert to an indoor itinerary. First I surf the web and check my emails at the Internet café, then I head back to the Hotel Alpina. The hotel has a number of picture books which keep me entertained. I get chatting to Jessie, one of the girls working at the hotel. She is great to chat with but sadly fails to deliver on a key item: a promised piece of apple pie!

In the evening, Jessie's boyfriend comes over from Leysin, a resort high up on the north side of the Rhone valley and famous for its International School of Mountaineering. We play cards and sink a few beers, and then I leave them to it and hit the sack. As I lie on my bunk, drifting off to sleep, someone decides to rest their hand on my foot as they stand chatting. I am less than impressed! A hot, stuffy night follows.

Tuesday 17ᵗʰ August

Travelling to Lausanne to meet old friend

I am on the move again today, quitting Zinal for Lausanne to meet up with a college (Bangor) friend who works at Lausanne university. From Lausanne I am to travel to Lauterbrunnen in the Bernese Oberland, to stay with life-long friends from Birkenhead who are holidaying in Switzerland this year. With some sadness I say goodbye to Nadia and her family, and to the happy Hotel Alpina, and walk past the dark brown chalets to the bus stop in Zinal.

The weather is dull. The bus journey to Sierre, however, is full of interest, especially the heart-stopping drops from the roadside to the gorge far below. I step off the bus at Sierre and warily check to see if my drunken acquaintance is still around (he isn't). I then rescue my second sack from its luggage locker (literally – I had failed to pay the correct amount when placing it there on the way through to Zinal and now had to barter with the attendants to have it released from incarceration) and then board the train for Lausanne.

Lausanne town centre rises with surprising, breathless steepness from the station. I cache my second sack at the station (this time paying the right amount) and head through the steep streets in search of food and entertainment. It is some hours before my friend is to meet me at the station on his way home from work, so after food I find an Internet café, where I spend a pleasurable hour sending and reading emails and catching up on the news. Then it occurs to me that as I have no sleeping bag, I will need a blanket or something to keep me warm when I camp with my Birkenhead friends in Lauterbrunnen. I wander the streets, find a suitable shop and manage to locate and buy a cheap blanket. As I stand and pay for this, I notice a shelf of English language books. My luck is in: *Death in Holy Orders* by P.D. James is there and I snap it up with glee.

Next I go to a café to grab a coffee and gloat on my good fortune. But my gloating is stopped dead. Across from me, on another table, sit an elderly couple: the man looks desperately thin and weak and can hardly stay awake, and my immediate impression is that he is terminally ill; his wife chats to him in the most dignified, beautiful way, being neither over-the-top with forced gaiety nor down-beat with the concerns that she must be feeling. I'm deeply touched.

Back at the station, I find a seat and settle down to people-watch and read my newly purchased book. Then with an hour still to go until my friend's scheduled arrival, I adjourn to the outside, to crouch under the eves of the station and watch on with interest as the Lausanne commuters struggle home through a violent thunder storm.

My friend Jerome duly arrives and it is a lovely meeting. We haven't seen each other since a trip to see Mike Lates (of 'Prague stag-do' fame) on the Isle of Skye back in 1995. Then, I was in poor shape having just arrived back from my year in Australia with no job, no money, no plan and (crucially) no confidence. We pick up with each other over a gorgeous meal, catching up on the big events, some happy, some very sad. Then we drive over to Jerome's flat about ten miles out of town, where I meet up with his wife Ann and chat some more while drinking a strong pear alcohol with a name I cannot recall (but whose taste I can... mmmm). I have a room to myself!

Wednesday 18th August

Travelling to Lauterbrunnen to meet Birkenhead friends

Breakfast next morning is a fun affair. The two boys, Axel and Oscar, are around and it is great seeing Ann and Jerome interacting with them. The weather is also much improved and I'm able to see the cracking view from the balcony. Jerome and I walk to the local Metro station where we board a train into Lausanne, he to get off at an early stop for the university, while I shall travel to the main-line train station. But it transpires that I am not deposited at the main-line station. To reach it, I must board a sort-of funicular that whisks me down the hill to the station proper. All a bit confusing. Anyway, things work out fine and I reach the main-line station and board one of those double-decker trains to Switzerland's capital city, Berne.

It is a captivating journey through soft, pastoral scenery. I am a little nervous about meeting up with Gary, Hazel and family (in Lauterbrunnen) because this was their holiday and I didn't want to invade their space. I resolve to join them for two days, which I feel satisfies my very real desire to spend time with them but not intrude too much on their wider holiday plans.

I've known Gary and Hazel (Birkenhead friends) for years, from my Venture Scout days. In fact, I've known Gary for longer as we were in the Scouts together. The Arrowe Venture Scout unit ('The Unit') was a mixed group of people in their late teens and early twenties, who met up one evening a week to do something instructive and then retire to a local pub. We rented a loft space ('The Hut') above a garage on the Craflwyn Hall estate between Beddgelert and Llyn Dinas in the Gwynant valley, North Wales. Often we had weekend walking trips based there. I recall it having a sloping floor which played havoc with your senses as you tried to cope with the effects of excessive alcohol consumption. Anyway, I am merely skimming the surface of a vast vat of happy memories. Alas, 'The Unit' fizzled out some years ago. Craflwyn Hall is now owned by The National Trust and 'The Hut' is part of the developments they have put in place... and to their credit they have turned this ageing, rhododendron-ridden

150

estate into something special. To this day, six of us, including Gary, still meet for a beer one night a week, and I count this small band amongst my best of friends.

As the train enters Berne, I can see the Bernese Alps, with their prime frontage occupied by that famous trio: the Eiger, Monch and Jungfrau. Also visible is a lot of graffiti on the track walls, but this is of such a high standard that I find it pleasurable. I then hop on a train along the beautiful Lake Thun, to the town of Interlaken. I've been to the Bernese Alps before, the last time being in 1986, but I have forgotten just how grand the peaks are: they seem to loom menacingly over the intermediate peaks and I am surprised and taken aback by their size.

Interlaken has modernised a lot since 1986. There is a supermarket complex near to the station, so I nip in for some shopping and a bite to eat. I then jump aboard the third and final train of the day. This passes through Wilderswil where a gang of us from 'The Unit', including Hazel, stayed back in 1980; then at Zweilutschinen, where a mountain spur splices the main valley into two, it takes the right-hand arm to the village of Lauterbrunnen, nestled beneath some seriously brutal precipices. (The other arm has Grindelwald at its head.)

I follow the now-familiar rigmarole of sorting my gear into needs and need-nots, and store the need-nots in a luggage locker. Then with my remaining sack and a shopping bag containing my newly-purchased blanket, I march out of town towards the campsite, a long and rather sweaty trek. The family tent is located, the car being the give-away. No-one is at home. I dump my sack in a spot that proclaims

'Martin has arrived', then grab a handful of washing and make for the toilet block to shower and wash some kit. It is there, some time later, that Gary's two lads (Mark and Nick) find me. We go back to the tent where I am plied with beer while awaiting mum and dad's arrival. Gary and Hazel duly arrive. It is just so lovely being with them and the two lads. There is lots of catching up to do, stories to tell and tales to hear, all against a background of woodlands and those dark, brooding cliffs and their cascading waterfalls. I even have my own room within the family tent.

Thursday 19th August

Lauterbrunnen: hiking to the Oberhornsee

Next morning I learn of two things: firstly, that it has rained overnight and so my washing of the previous day is as sodden as ever (its drying was to become a bit of an epic); and secondly, that the couple in the tent behind had had a bit of a bust-up, the sort best staged within the privacy of the home rather than a far-from-soundproof tent. I nip to the site shop to buy a map of the area. We study this over a breakfast of boiled eggs, bread and jam, and it is decided that we should drive to Stechelberg ('Stickleback') at the valley's head, for a walk into the hills.

Having parked up, we opt to walk to a lake called the Oberhornsee. Things start in a mellow sort of way; but then suddenly our route shoots up a brutally steep track through the woods, to which someone has added wooden steps just high enough to be a real pain. I toil along at the back, my progress embarrassingly poor when one considers that I've been walking here for some weeks and these guys have only just arrived. Gary and Hazel go to the gym regularly, I recall, so I make a mental note to do the same when I get settled after the trip. Eventually, this purgatory ends and we walk through a typical Swiss meadow with stunning views across the valley to the cliffs and snows of that most graceful of peaks, the Jungfrau. Now that I can breathe (!), I really start to enjoy myself. Our plan is to stop for lunch at a mountain hamlet called Obersteinberg. The hamlet comes into view and we reach it along a level track that curves around the hillside. It is washing day there too: white bed sheets hang to dry in the breeze, held in place by huge wooden clothes pegs; and taken together with the backdrop of the Jungfrau, the scene makes me think of prayer flags in the Himalaya.

After lunch (banana sandwiches) we head off for the second leg of the walk, which looks very promising indeed. And so it proves. The path winds along the grassy hillside, ducks down to cross a cold stream issuing from the glaciers above, and then begins a final, sinuous climb up a rocky prow to reach the basin holding the lake. The prow is gorgeous, both in its shape and location. We climb up it in steep, tight zig-zags, the gravely path broken up every so often with boulders between which sprout large-leafed greenery. I am in the middle now. The lads are ahead: they have less mileage on their clocks and are lean and fit. Gary and Hazel are behind and I can hear their chatter and footfalls on the stony path.

The lake itself is perhaps a bit of an anti-climax, small and ringed by a tide-mark of unattractive mud which suggests that it has dried out from its normal size. However, it is a stunning viewpoint for the surrounding peaks. I don't know the peaks in this area well, but two I do recognise: the Lauterbrunnen Breithorn further up the valley; and the ever-present Jungfrau whose cone of white appears over the lip of the basin cupping the lake. I walk up to this lip to see this peak's huge sweep of supporting crags and find to my joy that the cloud has dropped down beneath me, forming a bubbling sea of greyish-white that seems to crash like surf against the crags. We stay for a while and then decide it is time to go as the weather is clearly serving notice of its evil intentions.

On the way down, we stop on the bridge crossing the glacier torrent, to listen to its gurgling noises as it passes under a snow bridge. The blast of cold air acts as a wake-up call to the worsening weather. So the long descent continues. Part way down, our way is blocked by some cattle through which we pass (nervously!) to carry on. There is good talk, making the descent fun. But the weather has the final and loudest word: the rain falls strong and hard, and there are rumbles of thunder as we stride quickly down the valley track through the gloom and wet to the warm lights of Stechelberg and the car with the English registration plates.

Returning to the tent is like returning to 'The Hut'. We drink many mugs of tea and pore over our day's route on the map. Meanwhile, the rain increases in ferocity to biblical proportions. After tea, we play board games by the light of the gas lamp. Someone notices that the groundsheet in the awning where we are sitting is like a water bed. Rainwater has seeped under the tent and is collecting under the groundsheet. It is surely only a matter of time before it emerges through the peg holes to flood out the sleeping quarters. We grab a broom and start 'brushing' the unseen water back out towards the tent entrance. Half an hour of frantic activity ensues. While some sweep, others place belongings onto chairs and tables, or hang them from hooks on the tent poles. Some of our neighbours offer help; others just laugh and watch on with amusement. As my grandfather used to say, 'How many S's in 'lousy'; how many G's in 'buggers'. Eventually, the threat recedes and we retire to bed.

Friday 20ᵗʰ August

Lauterbrunnen: visiting Trummelbach falls

I'm up first and make tea. We are all tired and not really up for a fast start to the day, and it looks like the weather feels the same way: a grey, drippy gloom hangs over the valley. A large group of Australian Scouts and Guides are camped nearby. They've coped really well through the torrential rains of the night and are now packing up with admirable order.

After breakfast, we walk up the valley to the famed Trummelbach Falls. These are an incredible sight, especially after the heavy rains. A lift whisks us up to the top of the falls, from where there is a beautiful view back down the valley towards Lauterbrunnen and its symmetrical frame of cliffs. Today, the view is more akin to a jungle, what with the clouds wreathing the cliff faces and the stifling humidity. We follow a walkway into the mountain, to reach the falls, where we peer down and see the water thundering with indecent haste through the natural constrictions, like a hydro-electric plant trying single-handedly to meet national demand. The walkway descends down to the base, keeping close to the frantic water wherever it can. It is deafening but fantastic.

I laze away much of the rest of the day, sometimes chatting and sometimes reading. It is lovely to do nothing. Later, the others go off so I do some sorting around the tent and take the bottles back to the shop, to reclaim the deposit (for my friends – honest). We play games in the evening, listening as more rain falls, forming 'Lake Lauterbrunnen' yet again outside the tent, and so for a second time we end the night by sweeping the 'water-bed' groundsheet and relocating our gear to higher ground. My last memory as I drop off is of Gary sweeping out.

Saturday 21st August

Travelling to Fiesch

Today is the end of my time with Gary, Hazel, Mark and Nick. I've had a brilliant stop with them and am secretly very sad to leave. Anyway, I'm awake early so nip off to the shop to buy thank-you presents. When I get back, I make tea. Having drunk this I say my goodbyes. This marks the end of my trip, really. I am growing weary of solo travelling and just want to go home. But my return ticket is booked for three days hence, so I plan to make the best of this short time and go to Fiesch in the upper Rhone valley, to take the cable car up to the famed Eggishorn with its wonderful view.

I walk back to Lauterbrunnen, grab my spare gear, pick up the train and travel down to Interlaken where I have breakfast at the supermarket. Outside is a large car park with an inviting array of dustbins. A fly-on-the-wall camera would record footage of a guy (me) unpacking his gear onto the tarmac and then binning various items. This self-same footage would then show the guy approaching some innocent bystanders, proffering an aged blue karrimat, at which point they look back at him like as if he is a weirdo and remove themselves to a safe distance. The guy then bins the karrimat – all very odd. Well, yes, it may be odd, but at the end of the trip I embark on a new life and something in me wants to discard some detritus of the old. I feel good about the 'new life' because it involves a move back to Birkenhead and friends like Gary and Hazel.

So follows a train journey back along Lake Thun, over the Bernese Alps via Kandersteg and the Lotschberg Tunnel, to the Rhone valley and the ever-so-familiar Brig. Here I nip on a local train (the Glacier Express, no less) for the short hop further up the Rhone valley to Fiesch.

Fiesch is shut when I arrive. When the tourist information place opens, the people there are very kind and sort me a room at a sports complex on the edge of town. I walk to it with my full retinue of gear (and aching back) and check in. It is a soulless place, a sort-of college campus with a hint of prison mixed in, and not to my tastes. But it is clean and my bed is good and comfortable. I am the sole occupant in a large room with many such beds. Having got sorted, I ask the lady at reception about my boots and whether I need to stash them somewhere special. It isn't a happy conversation and it leaves me feeling awkward and petty.

I walk back into town to buy some food for tomorrow's trip up the Eggishorn. On my return, I reckon I should make use of the facilities that come with the room, one of which is access to the swimming pool. It is so lovely to have a swim. Steadily it dawns on me that the site is teeming with Scouts and Guides. I must be one of the oldest there. In the evening, I walk into town yet again, this time for a cheer-me-up pizza (a success) and to suss out when the cable car to the Eggishorn starts to run the next morning. My final act of the day, on my return to the complex, is to ask at reception if there is a bar on site, which gleans the response 'No' delivered in a stern, sober tone!

Sunday 22nd August

Fiesch: cable car trip to Eggishorn

My commute this morning is extremely pleasurable: two cable car rides; the first to Fiescher Alp (a small tourist complex and hamlet); and the second to a subsidiary summit of the beautiful Eggishorn. It is still early and breathlessly cold when I arrive. The main summit is perhaps half a mile away, down and up on a stony path that plays havoc with my long-suffering knees. There is an icy glaze on some of the rocks, a further impediment to my already stuttering progress. But sure enough, the small rocky top arrives. I clamber around amongst the summit rocks, taking in the full round of vista.

Here is one of the best views that I've ever seen, and justly famous. Its most photographed aspect is the view up the sweep of the Aletsch glacier (the moraines of which accentuate its curves and remind me of the rings of Saturn) to the back of the mighty Jungfrau and Monch and the rather down-trodden Eiger. Sometimes, when you have seen views in photographs, the reality can be disappointing, but this is not so now and I felt real elation at what I see. There is some peculiarity to the location of the Eggishorn, because despite its relatively modest height (a touch under 3000 metres), you can see an astoundingly large proportion of the alpine 4000-metre peaks from its top. I won't reel them all off, but most of the peaks around Zermatt (Matterhorn, Monte Rosa and so on) are visible, as are Mont Blanc and many of her attendants. Nearby, the Aletchshorn rears beautifully across the void. A stunning, stunning view.

As I sit in the sun, a girl arrives. We start to chat and share some food. Her name is Bridget and she is from Germany. Bridget is with her family and has headed up here on her own, leaving her father and younger brother back at the cable car station. Soon she leaves; I stay on, left to myself. When I get back to the cable car station, I see her again, this time with her family, and pop over to say hello. We chat some more. Hmmm. When it is time to go, she walks with me to the cable car station. Well, she seems physically very close and her skin isn't crawling with distaste at my proximity (oh self-confidence, where are you?) so I take a massive gamble and kiss her, first on the cheek and then properly! Good move. It's a lovely few minutes, a nugget of absolute pleasure that comes out of nowhere (these things never happen to me, to quote the old cliché). Eventually, we part company and I head down to Fiescher Alp.

At Fiescher Alp I go for a wander, then sit around, then go for another wander, then sit around some more, and then go for yet another wander, and finally have a coffee before taking the cable car down to the valley and the questionable delights of Fiesch.

I have so much to think about concerning the near future. I will go and stay with my parents for a week, and then move up to Birkenhead with minimal gear, to find somewhere to live and start up as a freelance technical author. And I will also need to be disciplined and start writing the book of the trip, which is to be called *Five Weeks One Summer*. I am longing to see family and friends but have real forebodings about what the return and start-up will be like, based on my poor experiences when I came back from Australia ten years previously.

That evening, I walk into Fiesch for some food and then head back to my empty room in the sports complex.

Monday 23ʳᵈ August

Travelling to Martigny

I decide to travel part way to Geneva, to the town of Martigny, and stop there overnight so as to be closer to Geneva airport for my flight tomorrow morning.

On the train to Brig, I sit opposite a mountain guide who is bound for Zermatt, where he is to meet up with a client. My introductory gambit is to point at his boots (as a precursor to asking if he is a mountaineer). Unfortunately, he thinks that I'm having a go about his boots being on the seat, so removes them but looks at me as if I'm a real pain. I get the drift, manage to clarify that I'm not trying to be a railway official, and with that sorted we chat amiably for the duration of the trip. My next train, from Brig to Martigny, stops everywhere. But as I have a whole day this does not matter. Eventually, we pull into Martigny and I alight and start searching for somewhere to stay. I opt for the hotel right by the station. Checking in is fine, but getting to the room is a slow affair because of the misbehaving lift. My patience ebbs away far too fast and I think the girl accompanying me understands some of my muttered curses.

The day is still young. I look into the possibility of taking a coach trip up to the Emosson dam, high up in the hills and some distance away, but it is costly and the timings feel all wrong. Instead I walk around Martigny, visiting an art exhibition and then a Roman amphitheatre where I am a privileged spectator to a cameo performance of a gladiator dual by two young girls (tourists, like me) to their parents who sit watching from the stone seating.

Late afternoon, I return to the hotel armed with an English-language newspaper. This I read and then attack its puzzles and crosswords with mixed results. But in truth I'm just killing time before the journey home. So I go out for a walk and a final meal out, treating myself to a beautiful dish of thin slices of raw beef that you cook yourself on a tin of hot coals, served by an equally beautiful waitress who watches with practised patience as I burn both myself and the prized meat. I feel strangely relaxed, this despite the uncertainties that face me on my return to Britain. There are fallen leaves on the pavement – time to go home.

Tuesday 24th August

Travelling home

I awake to thunder and lightning, and also to a broken wrist watch. Packing takes no time, nor does breakfast, and I soon find myself walking across the rain-sodden street to the railway station.

And so the final journey of the trip begins. Initially the train is empty and I am left to my thoughts. Then, as we head along the side of Lake Geneva, more and more people get on: rain-drenched commuters on their way to work. Suddenly, I'm no longer on a trip to the Alps, but back in the real world.

A final word

A week after my return to the UK, tragedy hit our family. My father fell ill very suddenly (from a blocked bowel) and after a couple of days of frantic efforts by the medics, he died from complications. My lack of future plans turned from a nuisance to a God-send, giving me the opportunity to live with my mum for a few months, looking after her while trying to start out as a freelance technical author. But truth is I've never been cut out to work on my own (the loneliness would be a living death), so when I saw a job advertised for a permanent technical author at a company near to Chester, I applied... and got it. I work there to this day (autumn 2009) and live in Birkenhead, where I was born.

Yes, autumn 2009. It's taken an embarrassingly long time to write this book! As I read through it for the umpteenth time, it all comes back to me. And of course I have the slides to remind me as well. Some observations of my own: I seemed to spend a lot of the trip eating; and I feel I could have done more during my first two weeks when I was in Zermatt. But I also note periods of intense happiness and activity, especially the spells in Saas Grund, Zinal and Lauterbrunnen. I still get into the hills, with my latest mountain challenge being to complete the Wainwrights. However, serious illness hit me very hard at the end of 2008 and though fitness returns, it isn't particularly quickly and my hill-walking expeditions have been on hold for a long while. But the day will come, pretty soon methinks, when I'm yet again standing by a summit cairn with a sweaty back, fumbling for my camera (I've gone digital now) and trying not to trip on the scattered stones.

And on that note I will say good-bye and thank you for reading even just this one sentence.

Martin E Block

Prenton, Birkenhead, November 2009

About the Author

Martin Edward Block was born in Birkenhead in 1963, the youngest of three children. He moved away in his early twenties, to live in various localities, but chiefly North Wales, only to return to Birkenhead in 2004. In 1997, after stints as a maths teacher and a research scientist, Martin settled in to his chosen career as a technical author, writing instruction manuals first for the petrochemical industry and then latterly for a technology company based on Deeside near to Chester, where he currently works. Mountains and mountain climbing have featured large in Martin's life from a very early age, and the years have seen him climbing extensively in Britain and further afield (especially the Alps which he loves). His walking boots and camera still get plenty of use, as do his long-suffering knees.